Rag Dolls
and
Plastic Horses

by
Robert G. Hobson

Bob Hobson has been a member of the board of directors of the Capernwray Missionary Fellowship of Torchbearers from the very beginning of the ministry in the United States. We have valued immensely the unfailing faithfulness with which, in many parts of the world, both with the spoken and the written Word, he has taught the vital, liberating truth of the indwelling presence of the Lord Jesus in the life of the believer.

Major W. Ian Thomas, D.S.O., T.D.
Founder of the Capernwray Missionary
Fellowship of Torchbearers

ISBN 0-939241-61-7

Foreword

Having accepted Christ as my Savior later in life, I was very fortunate to have had extremely good Bible teachers during the early years of my Christian experience. I was well aware that Christ died for me, took away my sins, and lived within me, but His indwelling presence was not real. Although I was growing spiritually, I was experiencing great difficulty living the Christian life. The harder I tried, the more I failed. My Christian life was not the joy that was promised...it was pure frustration and failure.

Five years after my conversion, I was working one summer at a Bible camp in Canada when I met Bob Hobson and heard his message of "the lordship of Christ in your life." As I listened over the week of meetings it finally became very clear to me that Christ really was alive and living within me in the person of His Holy Spirit. What a revelation! I now understood why I could not live the Christian life no matter how hard I tried. But Christ could, and only Christ, as He lived His life out through me! I also came to realize that Christ was not interested in my ability, my efforts, or who I was, only in my availability. This was life changing!

As I began to daily be totally available to Him, I began to see Christ live His life out through mine, and in the language of trust, of what He was going to do...said, "Thanks, Lord, it's going to be exciting to see what You are going to do through me." It was a fantastic reversal in my Christian life.

If you or someone you know are experiencing a similar frustration or failure in your Christian life, then this book is for you. It will provide you with the "how to" live the Christian life by allowing the indwelling spirit of Christ to live through you. Once you grasp this simple truth, it will revolutionize your Christian life! It did mine!

Dr. Conrad Milne, Ph.D.
New Mexico State University, Retired

Acknowledgments

It is with a sense of deepest gratitude that I express thankfulness and appreciation for not only their love and friendship, but for their input into this book:

To Jim and Brenda Watson; Clovis, California, for supplying the computer.

To Joy Shannon; Gold Beach, Oregon, for the impossible task of editing.

To Steve Randolph, for his computer skills in setting up the book.

Cover design and illustration by Fred Galloway.

Fred is a freelance artist residing in Greenwood, South Carolina, with his wife, Jennifer. Their two children, Ian and Amy, are the models for the painting on the cover. Through the years, they have enjoyed discovering more about Christ's indwelling life through Bob and Nina's ministry.

Fred received a BFA and MA in painting from East Carolina University. He has been painting open air landscapes for many years and his art is presently used for patterns in the textile industry.

Author's Note

My purpose in writing this book is meant to be a source of encouragement to those who have become a Christian, but have been and are struggling in their Christian life. As we will discover, it is one thing to become a Christian...it is quite another to live like the Christian we have become!

I have met so many discouraged, defeated, depressed...wonderful, lovely Christians who are simply tired of the "rat race." They have come to the conclusion that their discouragement, depression and disappointment is just the reality of the Christian life and it won't be any better until we see Jesus.

It is against this backdrop that I have endeavored to share the reality of the life which He gave us and for which He has made provision for the living of it. Does this mean we will never be disappointed again? Does this mean we will never be discouraged? That would be like "pie in the sky." It does mean, however, that we will never, ever *have* to live under the domination of such discouragement and disappointment. The question is...how does that work?

The intent of this book is that we will discover the sheer joy of Jesus Christ living through us the kind of life which we never could! He never expected that we could or would live the Christ life. Jesus was and is the only one that could and did live that life, for He is the one who has ever been...JESUS. No more than I could live your life...or you live my life. That would be impossible. So it is with the Christ life! He is the only one that can live it!

So be encouraged. If you have failed at the Christian life...and who hasn't; you have simply lived up to His fullest expectation of you. He knew you would fail. That is why He came...to do what you cannot do!

Now is your opportunity to discover and begin to enjoy all that He has provided...His very life!

Good reading...and great living!

Dedication

It is with the deepest sense of love and gratitude that I dedicate this book to my wife, Nina. For over 50 years she has been my loving companion, comforter, cheerleader, encourager, challenger, and above all, one who constantly exhibits the life of the Lord Jesus. Without doubt, a living example of the relationship which I describe in this book. Daily, she allows the Lord Jesus to demonstrate Himself through her to me. Thank you, Nina, for being available to Him...and to me.

Contents

Rag Dolls and Plastic Horses

The plane dipped its wing and there it was, the village of Hoskins, New West Britain, Papua New Guinea. I could not believe that I was on the mission field where my friends Ken and Stephanie Springsteen are missionaries along with their two youngest children, Faith and Joel. The three oldest were attending school in Goroka.

After lunch we were enjoying a bit of nostalgia regarding Stephanie's parents, when in the midst of our laughter, Joel came into the living room. With a rag doll under one arm and a plastic horse under the other, he declared defiantly, "These are mine!" Okay, who cares? I thought. We laughed, ignored him and went on with our conversation.

However, I could not help noticing the look on his face. Such a fiercely determined, willful look of arrogance for such a little boy. There was no doubt to whom the rag doll and plastic horse belonged. The impact of that statement still lingers in my mind. Who cares to whom they belong? To Joel they were valuable, and he certainly did not want any misunderstanding as to whom was the rightful owner.

A rag doll and plastic horse. Their value? Not much. Yet defiantly, Joel proudly declared ownership. There was no life in either of the two; that didn't matter. At that moment his whole life was wrapped in those two items.

Sound familiar?

We as Christians have our pet doctrines, evangelical clichés, theologies, denominations, evangelical phrases, hymns and choruses. Should anyone doubt their value, all one needs to do is to challenge us and we will hear along with Joel:

"These are mine! How dare you challenge the value of my personal 'evangelical' rag doll and plastic horse?"

What is the value of a rag doll and a plastic horse? There is no life in either. The rag doll could not speak or react. The plastic horse is unable to respond and certainly he couldn't ride it. But never mind.... "These are mine!" There is no truth in a rag doll and plastic horse, but nevertheless, "These are mine!"

Truth and value are unimportant to a three-year-old boy. What was important to him was ownership of two insignificant, lifeless objects. Ownership, not *relationship*. For a functional relationship to exist, there must be life from both sides. Otherwise it is not *relationship*, it is ownership of the worst kind.

The Lord Jesus did not die on the cross in order to provide for us a non-life or non-living relationship. He did not redeem us so that we in turn could pump out some nondescript, meaningless relationship to Him and to others; to program ourselves and others into a man-made system of so-called "religious" spirituality.

The fact is that the Christian life can be simply summed up as a conglomeration of all the above. We each have our own private "rag doll" and "plastic horse" that we value and trumpet as *the* "truth." We clutch the denominational rag doll to its death and ride that plastic horse as though it had life. We prop it up, program it, pump new blood into it, expecting it to come to life. There it stands, completely, absolutely lifeless; but so very precious to us. All in the name of a rag doll and plastic horse that we call the Christian life.

These are mine!

There's nothing quite as important as a rag doll and a plastic horse, if you are three years old!

2

It's Called "The Christian Life"

Anyone who is a Christian has heard from the very beginning that our relationship is a "personal relationship" with Jesus Christ. I must admit that for me, there wasn't much that was personal about it and here is the reason.

I was given to know, based on the fact of what Jesus Christ did for us in providing a personal relationship with Him *in* salvation, I was in turn, expected to do something *for* Him. Most of Christianity is based on the expression of doing "something *for* Christ," living *for* Jesus, doing something *for* Him. Each week we would hear another "rag doll" issue of being busy for Him. I saw a bumper sticker the other day, "Look busy, Jesus is coming." I know the feeling.

The evangelist would arrive for the annual "revival" meeting and what was called a "challenge to commitment." We were reminded that we had not witnessed enough *for* Him. We had not prayed enough, been faithful to the church, or hadn't given enough. We plead, "Guilty as charged!"

However, we go out with a renewed ambition and commitment to live *for* Him in a more consistent manner, to the best of our ability...only to discover that after the heat of the emotion, we are back at failure and guilt. What a rat race, and the cheese tastes terrible! Yet we call it "the Christian life."

At this writing, I am in a Bible Conference sharing the truths of the indwelling Lord Jesus. A lady came up to me afterward, her eyes full of tears. She said, "I almost didn't come this morning."

I said, "Oh, why was that?"

"I have been thinking all week, why am I here? What is the purpose of my life, as a Christian? Where am I going? I am such a failure. I just don't want to go and have more guilt heaped upon me for not having done as much as I could have *for* the Lord. I was just ready to quit. I am so glad I came. To realize that He, the Lord Jesus, lives in me and I don't have to perform on His behalf or on anyone else's behalf. I can hardly believe it, but it's true."

In the course of the week she progressively discovered that the Christian life is not *her* best effort on His behalf but *His* best effort through her as an available, redeemed loved one in Christ.

Have you ever made the liberating discovery that the Lord Jesus did not die on the cross in order to inflict pain in you because you didn't *do* enough? The reason He died *for* you was in order to *give* His life to you. Having given His life to you, He now lives *in* you for the purpose of living through you, to live through you the kind of life that you cannot live.

Within that package relationship are all the truths of sins forgiven, cleansing, and our destiny changed from hell to heaven. Praise the Lord for it all! But it was not His purpose for us to develop a systematized routine of a "rag doll and plastic horse" approach. These have no life. *He came to give life and that more abundantly, John 10:10.*

The Scripture is clear regarding the fact that we are "Dead in trespasses and sins." Paul states in Ephesians 2:1, "And you hath He quickened [made alive] who were dead in trespasses and sins." No questions about that.

The Scripture is equally clear that He came to give us the life that we do not have. A dead man has no need of being healed. What a dead man needs is life, and by virtue of His birth, life, death and resurrection, He gave us that life.

The disciples were in desperate need of life, even though they were in the presence of the One who is life. That is why He said to them in John 14:20, "At that day, you shall know that I am in the Father, and you in Me, and I in you." Astounding! The One speaking to them said, "I am going to come and live in you!"

The response from the disciples was a deafening, incredible silence. No response of any kind. Why? Because they had no understanding of what He had said. How could it be that a living, speaking person could die and be resurrected and then come and live in them? Impossible! Consequently, no response.

I would venture to say that 95% of Christendom has the same response as the disciples. We play with our evangelical toys and trinkets, our rag dolls and plastic horses in the name of Jesus. Doing all we can *for* Jesus, to the best of our ability. All the while oblivious to the fact that the One whom we are trying to serve is actually alive, living within us. He's waiting for us to be through with our efforts *for* Him, so that He can begin to demonstrate His life *through* us.

Our hymns and songs have taught us very thoroughly that we can hold His hand and be comforted with the fact that He is beside us. (They also proclaim He is in front of us so that we can follow Him around like a little puppy.) All the while ignoring the fact that He is within us to do what we can't do and be what we can't be.

In the midst of this chaotic scene is the deep sense of failure and guilt that is almost overwhelming. Add barrenness, and defeat, just to name some of our experience, and it's unbearable. However, we clutch our "rag doll and plastic horse," and call it "the Christian life."

We hear another sermon on "How to be saved." Another sermon that says, "Those who aren't saved are going to hell!" Some people respond with a muted "Amen," but deep inside we yearn for the reality of that life which He promised. Only we stand and sing another verse of "Give of Your Best to the Master," or listen as someone solos, "I wonder, have I done my best for Jesus?"

5

Inside I scream, "I don't have to wonder if I have done my best for Jesus, I tried and it wasn't good enough! My best has never been good enough. I have tried and tried and failed miserably." By that time the benediction is being given, "Go with us as we go to our homes," and the final "Amen" has been uttered. Out we go, unaware that He is within, having promised that He would never leave us nor forsake us; never mind that incredible truth! Out we go for another week of doing the best we can, facing the reality that we are not adequate and consequently facing another week of failure and defeat.

It's called "the Christian life!" It is another week living "under the pile" all the while clutching the rag doll and plastic horse. Incredible!

In the midst of all that come the deep trials of life, trials that have no answers. Pain that nothing can soothe. The question arises, "Where is God?" and heaven is silent. "I have done my best, I have given it my best shot, and where is God?" No answer from God. Someone shouts at us, "Tough it out! Keep on keeping on!"

It's called "the Christian life," remember?

Do you remember when you came to know the Lord Jesus as your Savior? That day when you invited Him to come into your life and in so doing, He forgave you of your sins with the promise of life everlasting. Not just duration, but the life of God Himself. You were so excited, thrilled and overjoyed with the reality of what had happened. That joy was unspeakable, beyond definition. As the years have come and gone, what has happened to the "joy"? That joy that you once knew, so fresh, so real, vibrating so dynamically through your life that others wanted to know what you knew. What happened?

I heard a TV evangelist say recently, "If you have lost the joy of your salvation it is because you have strayed. You stopped going to church regularly. You stopped at a local bar and had a drink with the boys. You used a word or two of profanity and slow, but sure, you lost the joy." Indeed, that could happen.

What about the trustworthy Sunday school teacher, the dedicated deacon; the faithful parents that made sure that the family never missed Sunday school and church? They served on nearly every committee, even the committee of committees. They did everything in the church including doing the church bulletin, and cleaning the church every week as a volunteer for Jesus; only to be severely criticized by someone who had not helped with any of the work. What about that faithful servant who, working *for* Christ to the best of his ability, little by little burned out, coming to the conclusion, "It isn't worth it, I'm outta here"?

I know the answer to that dilemma because I've been there, done that, read the book, saw the movie, and bought the T-shirt. I was taught and programmed that the Christian life was me doing all that I could do to the best of my ability and it wasn't enough.

It is called "The Christian life!"

We have been told, "This is what the Christian life is about and I must continue to the best of my ability with no end in sight except the rapture and heaven." I wish He would hurry up and come, I can't take it much longer.

Is this the Christian life that God intended? Is there an answer to this dilemma? Can there ever be anything different than this constant trial, effort, failure and guilt?

I met a Bible college friend, many years after both of us had graduated, and he shared the following account with me. "Bob, I have been busy for Christ since I entered the pastoral ministry. I have been so discouraged and defeated. One day, I had come to the end after nearly 15 years of struggle for Jesus. I went down to the water's edge and just before I slipped into the deep water, I thought I had better have one last talk with the Lord, if He was there and if He was interested. I wasn't sure of either. I remember saying, 'Lord, You know I love You, I gave You my life. I have been laboring here in this church these past 15 years. I have done all that I know how to do and have failed miserably. I am really sorry about that. I thought I could do it, but I see now that I can't. I am a complete failure. Please forgive me for taking my life, but it is all that I can think of to do to end this misery and failure.' "

He went on to say, "Bob, I know that God doesn't speak audibly to people, but it was as real as though He did. That soft, still voice of the Spirit said to me, 'Jack [not his real name], what are you troubled about?'"

He said, "Lord, I am such a failure, the church hasn't done anything. There hasn't been anyone to come to know You in the past several years. Every program I have started has ended in failure. The people are angry with me and each other, and I can't take it any longer."

The Spirit continued, "Jack, whose church is this?"

He thought a moment and answered, "Lord, it is Your church."

"If it is My church, then why don't you let Me worry about it? Don't you know that I am not the least bit impressed with your energy and ability? Don't you realize My Son gave His life to you and that I now live *in* you because I want to live *through* you? My life being lived through you is not dependent on how clever you are, but dependent only upon Who I am *in* you? Don't you know that?"

"Then, Lord, You're not interested in my ability, but my availability?"

"Of course! I know that you can't live My life. I never said you could. I never expected that you would, because I knew you couldn't. But I can, and I will, if you will just let Me."

Jack said, "Bob, that conversation was just as real as the one you and I are having right now. It suddenly dawned on me the Christian life was not my doing what I could for Christ, but what He could do in me and through me, and that has completely changed my life!"

That's an incredible story. It has been multiplied again and again in the lives of people who make the simple discovery that the Lord Jesus lives within. The Christian life is not me doing my best, but it is Christ doing what He wants to with me, as well as what He wants to do in and through me.

When he made that discovery, did that mean his problems were over? Of course not, they had just begun. However, now because he knows that the Lord Jesus is living within him, he has the privilege of another dimension of trust. The anticipation of all that He is going to do within and through him as he goes about his daily routine of life, knowing that all the while the Lord Jesus is in charge and completely adequate for every situation. He no longer has to try and impress God with his own ability and needn't be concerned about others ready to criticize him because of his lack of ability, and he is free!

Do you know anything about that kind of freedom? You can, and I trust you will as you read on.

3

Just Have More Faith . . . Trust God

Ah, but of course, someone says, "All you need to do is have faith, just trust the Lord."

A friend who is at this writing attending seminary, asked me recently, "How does faith work? What is trust? How does trust work?"

He said, "I am a student in seminary and we were discussing faith and trust, and I asked the question of how does one balance faith and trust. No one had an answer for me." Here is a seminary student, studying to become a pastor or missionary, asking how to balance faith and trust and no one knew what faith and trust was all about.

In the first place, where is the biblical statement of having to balance faith and trust? Needless to say, my friend was deeply disturbed.

He went on to say, "I have a relative that has just left a religious drug rehab center. The reason for leaving? They were telling him that for his problem, all he needed to do was to have more faith. 'Trust the Lord, brother, you needn't have all these problems. Just have more faith.' "

His response was the same as my friends response, "How does that work? What is faith? What is trust? How does trust work?" He had to admit he didn't know.

The seminary professor couldn't tell my friend what faith and trust are, or how either of them worked in his life. He in turn couldn't tell his relative how they worked. Nobody knew, so it wasn't surprising that his relative said good-bye to the rehab center. Nobody knew!

Isn't it amazing that we have been hearing the same admonition for years and years, "Have more faith, we just need to trust God more," and it seems that no one can tell us what faith and trust is, much less how they work.

In the first place, the balancing of faith and trust is not the issue. We need to find out what faith is and what trust is. Perhaps we would be able to find what faith is by finding what it is not.

Faith is not that inner exercise whereby we try to muster a spiritual, touchy-feely, fuzzy emotion. When we "feel" that emotion that seems like we are in tune with God, or as they say, "We feel much closer to God." When everything just seems to "feel" right. Some now call it "the anointing." The anointing never seems to be evident until there is an emotion in a church or prayer service. We are told that "I am under the anointing," totally governed by the "feeling." That is not what faith or trust is!

Faith is the relationship between God and a person, made possible by the One who died for me, the Lord Jesus. By virtue of His dying for me, He now has given His life to me. He now lives *in* me for the purpose of living His life *through* me. He establishes that relationship the moment I invite Him into my life. As I discover the reality of who He is, among many other attributes, He is absolutely faithful. I have the privilege of trusting Him, and the language of trust is, "Thank You!"

For example: You have a well-known and trusted friend, and this friend says he is going to do something for you. How do you express your trust in him that he will do what he says he will do? Is it the process of pleading and asking him to do what he already said he would do? Naturally not, that would be ridiculous. If he is a real friend, one in which the relationship has been thoroughly tested and tried through the years, and he has been found worthy of trust, you would look at your friend and simply say, "Thank you."

Even so, the Lord Jesus has given countless promises of what He is and what He would do. Rather than say "Thank you," we continue to plead (pray) and ask to the point of embarrassing Him, trying to get Him to do what *we* want, instead of anticipating and expecting that *He* will do what He said He would do.

If the relationship with and in Christ is valid and real, we can quite simply say, "Lord Jesus, I am not really sure what this situation is all about. One thing I am sure of is that You are alive and live in me and I thank You for how You are going to handle this situation. Thank You very much!"

When I was pastor of a church, one of our members called one Sunday afternoon and related the story of a friend of his who had decided that he was going to quit the church he had been attending for many years. He asked his friend, "Why?"

"Because it is useless. I have done everything in my power to try to be the trusting, believing Christian that I know I should be. I have tried to be a good witness. I have passed out thousands of tracts. I have witnessed to as many as possible while on the job. The harder I try the more I fail, so I am giving it up."

My friend then called me that Sunday afternoon to let me know he was coming to church that Sunday evening. After the service I was introduced to this individual and he said to me, "Would it be possible for you to come to our home tomorrow evening?"

I said, "Of course, I would be delighted to come."

I arrived on their doorstep the next evening and this is the story he told me. "I have been a Christian for 20 years. I have done all that every preacher told me to do. I have tried to have more faith, I have tried to exercise more trust. I have tried to witness for Christ at every possible moment. I have passed out tracts at work to the point that everybody avoids me. I am embarrassed to go to work, and up until last night I was ready to quit church and tell God I am not interested anymore. I have done my best and apparently it is not good enough and I don't know what to do."

I shared with Bill (not his real name), the thrilling truth that the Lord Jesus was alive *in* him and it was now his privilege to tell Him that he was available to Him for whatever He wanted to do. I encouraged him to leave his tracts at home and live in that attitude of trust that says, "Thank You, Lord Jesus, for what You are going to do. I don't care whether You do anything or not, it's Your business. I just want You to know that I am available and I thank You."

In a flash, he knew that the Christian life was not his responsibility, but his availability to the One adequate for the task. It was *His* business, period.

We had a cup of coffee together and a bite to eat and I left.

The next afternoon he called me and asked, "Can you come over right away? I must talk to you." It sounded urgent to me so I dropped everything and went immediately to his house. I was met by him and his wife and he told me this story.

"I drove to work this morning telling the Lord that I was available to Him. I didn't know what He was going to do, it didn't matter. I said, 'Lord, I am just excited about the fact that You are alive and living *in* me and if I never know anything more than that, it is enough. I have never been more thrilled and happy as a Christian. Thank You, for what You are going to do.' "

In the middle of the morning, I was busy at my work and somebody passed by and said, "Hi, Bill. How ya doin'?"

I answered, "Fantastic!" and kept on working.

The guy stopped at my machine and engaged in a little talk and all of a sudden said, "What in the world has happened to you?"

I said, "I don't know. What do you mean?"

"You are different, what happened?"

I responded, "I can't talk to you now, but if you want to know, I'll see you at lunch on the dock."

"Great, I'll be there."

Lunchtime came and I headed for the dock to have my lunch, and sure enough, here comes the guy who wanted to talk.

Bill interjected, "Pastor Bob, keep in mind that I have never led anybody to Christ in all these years. No one would talk to me because I was so obnoxious. Now, here is one of my fellow workers wanting to know what had happened to me and I am scared out of my wits!"

Bill continued, "We sat down on the dock and immediately he said, 'Okay, what's happened?' "

I said, "You are not going to believe what I am going to tell you."

"Really?"

"Really!"

"Well, try me!"

"Last night I discovered Someone who has changed my life!"

"Yeah?"

"Yeah."

"Who is it?"

"His name is Jesus."

"Yeah, really? I don't understand that."

"I told you you wouldn't understand."

Bill went on to tell me with tears streaming down his face, "For the first time in my life, I had the joy of introducing another person to Jesus Christ. This, after I decided to quit and just tell Him that I was available. It is hard for me to believe."

Bill called me for several days in a row to let me know what had happened that day at work. He continued to tell me, "It is unbelievable," and from a human perspective it was.

Faith and trust are the ingredients of an incredible relationship between the Lord Jesus and a redeemed sinner. How exciting!

What do you suppose that the Lord would like to do with you? You, the one reading this page. What does He want to do with you, not what does He expect you to do for Him. Rather, what do you suppose He would like to do through you? The same thing as he did with Bill? Probably not, however, the principle is the same.

He is alive, living in you and just waiting for you to *quit*! Stop trying to do *for* Him what only He can do. By virtue of the fact that He lives *in* you, it follows that He would like to do *through* you what only He can do, whatever that may be.

The challenge is for you to just stop for a moment and acknowledge His indwelling presence and say, "Thank You, Lord Jesus, for living IN me. I haven't any idea what You would like to do through me, but thank You, go right ahead and do what You like." This is simply an expression of faith and trust in the "One" Who is adequate, in the presence of all our inadequacies!

Be careful if you pray a prayer like the one above, He is listening.

4

How Does That Work?

America is great in coming up with one-liners, commercials on TV, for example. "Meet the Press" had one that said, "We bring good things to life!"

Canon office equipment says, "When the rest says you can't, Canon says you can."

Hoover vacuum says, "Nobody does it like you!"

Red Dog beer declares, "You are your own dog." What in the world does that mean? Doesn't have to mean anything except *you're* the one that matters, *you* are the one in control.

Bud Lite beer says, "Won't fill you up...never lets you down." Never mind the fact that you'll get stoned out of your head, "It won't let you down." People buy various products based on commercials like these.

United Airlines makes a point that you should, "Fly the friendly skies of United," inferring that the skies are not friendly to any other airline.

Burger King said for years, "Have it your way." I went with some guys one day into a Burger King and feeling rather generous said to them, "I'll take care of this." Whereupon the girl behind the counter, obviously her first day on the job said, "May I help you?"

I asked, "Yes, is the commercial true?"

She looked at me rather puzzled and confused. About that time the manager came by and questioned, "Is there a problem here?"

I said, "No, I just asked her if the commercial is true." He had a sort of glazed look on his face. I repeated the question and quoted the Burger King commercial, "Have it your way."

He responded with a huge smile and said, "Yes, of course!"

I said, "Great, my way is free!"

Upon hearing that, he was quick to respond, "That isn't what the commercial means!"

"But that is what the commercial says." It looked like a stand off. I finally said to the manager, "Just joking." He didn't think it was funny. I thought it was hilarious.

In the movie, "The Lion King," the little lion says at one point, "I just can't wait to be king." Isn't that the truth? None of us can wait to be king. We all want to be king of our territory and will go to great lengths to assure ourselves of that kingship.

As little Joel exclaimed, "These are mine!"

Christianity is loaded with "one-liners," and for the most part they are accepted as gospel. It doesn't matter if they are true or not, we just accept them, probably without thinking. I mentioned earlier the hymn, "Give of Your Best to the Master." Someone says, "Well, of course, we wouldn't want to give anything less than our best."

What is our best? Did Jesus die in order to expect us to perform on His behalf with our very best? How does that work?

The prophet Isaiah speaks to that issue in the sixty-fourth chapter and the sixth verse, "But we are all as an unclean thing; and all our righteousnesses are as filthy rags." Notice what it doesn't say. It doesn't say that all of our sins are as filthy rags, but all of our "righteousnesses." The very best of us. The very best of what we are capable of being and doing.

Jeremiah also speaks in 17:9: "The heart is deceitful above all things, and desperately wicked." What is the heart? Well, it isn't that organ in your chest that keeps beating and keeps you alive.

As a young boy growing up in church, I would sing with my hand pressed against my chest, "Into my heart, into my heart, come into my heart, Lord Jesus." I had no idea what that meant. No one had ever explained what the heart was. We were given to know that it was our heart in our body, and I could never figure that out.

That isn't our heart. The heart is the real me living inside my body. It's the real me, and the real me is deceitful above all things and desperately wicked. Which is a nice way of saying, "I am rotten to the core and viciously wicked beyond comprehension."

Yet we sing, "Give of your best to the Master"? He didn't die for us in order for us to give Him our best. He died for infinitely more than that.

However, we try to satisfy our longing to be close to Him by singing, "Give of your best to the Master." That will be soothing perhaps, but sadly, it will miss the purpose of not only His death, but His resurrection life being lived out through us.

A young couple from Iowa were in the audience listening as I preached. I shared about the fact that the Lord Jesus was living in us and wanted to live His life out through us. They became very interested and some time later I had a conversation with the young man. He began to relate to me some of the age-old Christian one-liners: "You just have to let go and let God."

I said, "Great, how does that work?"

He thought a moment and continued with another, "Well, it's a matter of having faith and trusting God."

I said "Great, how do you do that?"

After a while, he said to me, "I hate that question, 'How does that work?' " Most people hate it because they do not know the answer.

Another well-known one-liner for someone going through some great trial: "Just remember, Romans 8:28 is still in the Book." A few years back, I was going through a tremendous trial. The wife of a very dear couple came up during a conference in which I was speaking and gave me that "one-liner," "Just remember, Romans 8:28 is still in the Book."

19

My response was, "I know that Romans 8:28 is still in the Book. That's not the problem. The problem is how do you get it out of the Book and into my life? That's the problem." She couldn't answer that question.

Another one-liner, "Just remember that God sees when the sparrow falls." A lady said that to me during that same crisis period of my life.

I responded by saying, "Is that supposed to help me? If it is supposed to help, I must admit that it doesn't."

She asked, "Why?"

I said, "Did you ever notice in that passage, that the Lord said He knew when the sparrow falls, however, He didn't help the sparrow live or come to its assistance? He simply let it fall, and knew when and where it fell. He didn't help the sparrow at all." She just looked at me in utter disbelief that I would say such a thing.

The fact is, He didn't help the sparrow, He didn't come to its aid. He didn't bring relief to the sparrow, He didn't rescue it from its dilemma. He let it fall and die. So much for help and comfort. Why He didn't do anything to help and comfort the sparrow is His business. I don't question why He did what He did, or how He did it, but it certainly was of no comfort to the sparrow. Some would look at that and be very upset by the fact that God didn't intervene on the sparrow's behalf.

Sometimes He doesn't intervene on our behalf. Have you noticed that? People get angry at God because He doesn't respond to their every snap of the finger, usually called prayer. They wonder why He doesn't get up off His throne and do something. Because He doesn't do something very personal they get angry at God and whine, "I'm disappointed with God." Entire books have been written on the subject.

In that moment of disappointment and anger, they forget all about the birth, life, death, burial, and resurrection of the Lord Jesus, and are totally consumed with their problem. They're unaware that the One who died for them is now resident within them though not necessarily for the purpose of springing to their aid at the snap of a finger, to physically intervene and supersede the physical laws that He set in order. He lives within for the purpose of demonstrating His life, peace, and joy in us in a manner that is beyond our wildest imagination. Paul the apostle calls it, "The peace that passes understanding," that is, beyond our comprehension.

All we are interested in is our well-being, our desires, and our wishes. We want it our way, *now*! When we don't get it, the only Christian thing to do is to whine and complain to as many as will listen. Call the prayer chain and enlist their help trying to get God to do what we want Him to do, *now*!

Scott Wesley Brown wrote a song, "When Answers Aren't Enough," and it goes like this,

"You have faced the mountain of desperation,
you have climbed, you have fought, you have won.
But this valley that lies coldly before you,
casts a shadow you cannot overcome.
And just when you thought you had it all together,
you knew every verse to get you through.
But this time all the sorrow broke more than just your heart,
and reciting all those verses just won't do."

Then the chorus,
"When answers aren't enough there is Jesus,
He is more than just an answer to your prayer.
And your heart will find a safe and peaceful refuge,
when answers aren't enough, He is there."

When answers aren't enough, there is Jesus. How does that work? How does He work? That is what we want to find out, not just factually, but functionally.

21

5

Is God Deaf?

That question, if not ridiculous, is most certainly irreverent. However, the way we pray would seem to indicate that He is either deaf, ill, on vacation, or dead. I can understand the "God is dead" movement a few years ago.

It would seem that He is "one of the above" to listen to us pray. I saw a bumper sticker that said, "Life is short, pray hard." My immediate response was, "What does that mean? What are they saying? How does one *'pray hard'*?" Do you grit your teeth and clench your fists? Do you work yourself into a frenzy to the point of soaking a handkerchief?

Assuming the position as pastor of another church, among the many meetings was the midweek prayer and Bible study. It was my responsibility to lead the Bible study and afterward, all of us, usually seven or eight people, would drop to our knees on a very hard floor and proceed to pray. Everyone was expected to pray. One by one each would voice their petitions and requests to the Lord, then finally I would close with the final prayer. This went on for several weeks.

I noticed as I listened to them pray that everyone was saying essentially the same thing. This bothered me. After a couple of months of this, I asked the group just before we went to prayer,

"How many of you think God is deaf?" The people were stunned by such a question. Not one hand appeared. I asked it again, "How many of you think God is deaf?" Not a single hand. Finally, someone dared suggest that He was not deaf, on the contrary His hearing was excellent.

Upon hearing that I asked, "Why then when we pray, do we all pray about the same thing?" (With some slight variation from someone a little more clever than the others.) No one dared to venture an answer to my question.

I said, "Tonight we are going to do something a little different. I am going to be the only one to pray. You can relax, you will not have to worry about what you're going to pray about." (A little suggestion here: if you ever have to pray publicly along with a lot of other people, be sure to be the first one to pray. If you wait, and are the last to pray, you will find that by that time all the good and spiritual phrases will have been used up. You will be left to either come up with something new, a little different, or bite the bullet and say the same things that other people have prayed. That could be very embarrassing).

Before we went to prayer, I asked all present to please listen very carefully to what was being said. If anyone was in agreement, express that affirmation to the Lord by a very quiet "amen" or "yes," inaudible if need be or audible, whatever.

I began to pray slowly, deliberately expressing our confidence and trust in Him who is adequate for the various situations of which we all were aware. It was absolutely incredible! There was a oneness of spirit, of love, joy, peace the likes of which I had never experienced before. How long I prayed I have no idea. When I finally finished the presence of the Lord was so real that no one dared speak. From that moment on, that was the format of our midweek service which grew to 500 and 600 people. That was the midweek Bible study and prayer service. Absolutely amazing!

Is God deaf? Of course not. If that is true, then why *do* we pray as though He were deaf? Why not pray as if He were alive and hearing, as though He meant what He said when He spoke in the Scriptures? Why not find out that He is trustworthy and with confidence talk with Him as though He were, and is, and will be? Why don't we pray with confidence, knowing that He is trustworthy? For the simple reason we don't have that confidence. We don't really believe that He is trustworthy. We have been too busy with ourselves, our own desires, wishes, plans, ideas, and opinions, our "rag dolls and plastic horses." As Charlie Brown would say, "Good grief!"

We all know the prayer procedure. The process of thanking Him for all the blessings that He has "bestowed" upon us, and I am thankful. We ask Him to bless this person and that person, and naturally, "Lord, we pray that you will be with them in a special way," as though His indwelling presence didn't exist. "Lord, go with us to our homes and bring us back tonight, safely," and very few show up "tonight." It is very disheartening to come back to church on a Sunday evening with so few people after we prayed so diligently for God to bring us back, safely. It would appear that He didn't bring many back, much less safely.

You see, it really doesn't matter how many people come back "tonight." What matters is the Lord Jesus! What matters is that He is not only alive, but living in us! We have the joy of living in eager anticipation of all that He wants to do with us and in us and ultimately through us! We get all tangled up in prayer and so many unanswered prayers that most never get past just a little child's "table prayer" and a "go to bed prayer."

Why Don't We Number Our Prayers?

That's a great idea. Think about it for a moment. If we were to number our prayers, God would know all the numbers. We could write the prayers out in detail perfectly, so that everything was said properly from a biblical point of view, even in the proper grammar.

We could have prayers to be said at mealtime. Rather than asking to "Bless this food to our bodies and us to Thy service," or "Bless the hands that have prepared the food," we could just utter a number!

As a small boy growing up in a very Christian home, I never could figure out why people asked God to "bless the hands that prepared the food." I remember looking at the person's hands that had cooked the meal and they didn't look very blessed to me. Seemed to me that somebody should have prayed for the rest of her body! It looked to me like it needed a lot of extra blessing, but then what does a small boy know? As a matter of fact, I still think that when I hear someone pray that prayer.

Think how easy it would be the next time you went out to eat, the restaurant is crowded, your meal comes and what to do? The whole family is there, everyone is watching, the kids are wondering what is going to happen. Wouldn't it be great at that point if we could just utter a couple of numbers. "Family, let us bow our heads. Dear Lord, number three and seven." The family would be instructed as to what the numbers meant and of course, God would know because He is omniscient. How simple it would be!

However, if you are ever out to eat by yourself and the waitress serves your meal, what then? I have watched people. Some scratch their eyebrows, others massage their sinuses and everyone knows what is going on. They are having their little prayer before they eat. No problem, just number your prayers!

A friend of mine said to me one day as we were discussing this subject. "I have it all figured out."

I said, "Really, what do you do?"

He explained, "I drop a napkin on the floor and pray on the way up!"

We had a good laugh, but it sounded like a good idea to me, although I have never tried it.

Seriously, how do we handle this issue? Have you ever thought of the simplicity of just unashamedly saying to Him, our living, indwelling Lord, "Lord Jesus, I love You, I praise You for living in me and I thank You for this tremendous demonstration of your provision," or simply, "Thank You, Lord Jesus."

There have been some occasions when there has been such a massive, long prayer begging for God's blessing on the food, I wondered what was in it. I thought I should wait and watch what would happen to others if they ventured so far as to eat it. I suppose, however, it was a demonstration of spirituality and prayer on my behalf. If it was, I wasn't impressed, except negatively.

No, there is no need to number our prayers. However, if our manner of praying is constant begging and pleading for God to do something on our behalf, we might as well number them and be done with it.

Oh, the simplicity of praying. Children know all about that. I was invited into the home of a lovely couple to have lunch along with their two children, one of which was still in the high chair. The older child whose name was Gary, asked his dad if he could pray. The younger one indicated that she wanted to pray also.

The father then asked the little one to pray and she made some verbal noises as a little non-speaking child would. I'm sure the Lord knew what she was talking about. Then Gary, who was three or so, began to pray. He said, "Thank You, Jesus, for this," he paused, looked up at Dad and said, "Dad, what is this stuff?"

Dad said, "That is beef Stroganoff."

The little guy continued, "Thank You, Jesus, for the beef Stroganoff." He looked over at the bowl of beans and said, "Thank You for the beans." He then looked at the salad, paused for a moment, and said, "Amen." Then he looked me square in the eye and said, "I don't like *saddad* [salad]." I loved it! So honest, so simple, so childlike. It would be, coming from a child!

Another instance finds a little three-year-old girl being told by her mother, in the presence of several friends who had gathered in their home after church, "Honey, it is time for you to go upstairs and get ready for bed."

She said, "Okay," and off she went up an open staircase at the end of the living room. In a few minutes, she appeared on the staircase. A vision of loveliness dressed in her pajamas, her long blond hair flowing regally over her shoulders. When everyone saw her, the talking stopped. When it was quiet she said, "I'm going up to say my prayers now, anybody want anything?" There was a good laugh, but unfortunately, that's what prayer means to most people.

No, absolutely never, is there a need to number our prayers. But wouldn't it be wonderful if we knew *Him* well enough that we could, moment by moment, communicate with the One who is indwelling us, sharing in that life which He died to give us, living moment by moment in the utter exhilaration and excitement of all that He is, and consequently of all that He wants to produce, not just within us, but through us? How exciting!

"Hobby, It Doesn't Work!"

A number of years ago I met a dentist in Calgary, Alberta. As a matter of fact, I had the joy of staying in their home for a week as I preached a series of meetings in their church. As the week progressed, my good friend Marshall began to make the discovery that the Lord Jesus was actually alive and living within him. To say that he was excited would be an understatement! The simplicity of saying to the Lord Jesus, "Lord, thank You for coming to live in me, and I place my life at Your disposal. My deliberate choice is I am going to trust You, and the expression of my trust is 'thank You.' Thank You in advance for all that You are going to do, not only in me, but through me to those with whom I come in touch."

I came back a year later and Marshall picked me up at the airport. I sensed immediately that something was wrong. We went through the normal greetings, "Hi, how are you doin'? How's everybody?" etc. We got in the car and headed home. I said, "Marsh, how are you getting along?"

With a look of unbelievable sadness he said, "Hobby, it doesn't work." I thought for a moment wondering what "it" was that didn't work. He finally said to me that all he had discovered the year before about Christ in his life, and working through his life was the great "it." "It" didn't work.

31

I sat silent for a moment and finally said, "Yes, I know, I understand what you are saying." I continued, "I noticed that you weren't at the funeral."

He questioned, "What funeral?"

I replied, "God's funeral. Didn't you get the notice? Everyone that I have ever known was there. We were notified by the angelic post office that God had died and the funeral was scheduled for a certain day and time. I was there, we were all there. Billy Graham was sitting in the front row, but I noticed that you were not there."

He sat rather stunned for a moment and finally blurted out, "God didn't die, there was no funeral! Hobby, what are you talking about?"

I told him, "Marsh, you just said that 'it' didn't work; referring to the Lord Jesus, residing in your life. By the way, I have never referred to Jesus as an 'it,' He is not an 'it,' He is the Lord Jesus. He is the second Person of the Godhead, and He is the One residing in you. So, if He is not doing anything in your life, I can only conclude that He is either dead, sick, or on a holiday; or for some reason has forgotten all about you and is not the slightest bit interested in you, so you might as well get used to it."

Marshall's response to all of that was to be expected. He knew the obvious, God was not dead, on vacation, or ill. "I know all of that, what is the problem?"

I explained to Marshall that his part of the relationship with and in the Lord Jesus is to remain available to Him, totally at His disposal with that attitude of gratitude which says, "Lord Jesus, it doesn't matter what You do in my life. All that matters is the fact that You are alive in me and anything You want to do with me, in me, or through me is Your business and I will be happy with what You do or don't do, and hilariously happy with *You*, thank You."

"Marshall, the burden of proof then is upon Him and you can rest. Enjoy your life, your wife, and family, while having a whale of a time on the way to heaven without having to go through hell to get there! Your problem, Marsh, is that you put your nose in His business."

"Thanks, Hobby, you're right," he responded. We had a great time of prayer together, just a time of praising the Lord that the Christian life is His business and, "Lord, it is going to be interesting to see what You do."

A few months later, the house next door to Marshall's was put on the market. In a few days time, a "sold" sign appeared. The new owners arrived and to their surprise, a black couple had bought the house. It turned out that the husband was a defensive tackle for the Calgary Stampeder football team. A man of huge proportions, some six feet eight inches tall and three hundred pounds. It turned out that the new neighbor was a Christian!

In the process of getting to know their new neighbors, Marshall had the joy of sharing some of what he had discovered about the Lord Jesus and His indwelling presence. The man became excited about a truth that he had never heard before, and asked Marshall if he would be willing to teach a Bible class made up of Calgary Stampeder football players.

Now who do you suppose planned that? The evangelism committee? Not a chance. Only God could have put that together. It is almost like God knows what He is doing, and of course, He does! He is just looking for some people through whom to have it happen. People who are prepared to come from the mind-set of, "These are mine," to the heart-set of, "These are His."

To further illustrate the point, a fellow by the name of Carl Luebke, along with his wife, Audrey, started coming to our church. He really came alive in the truth that the Lord Jesus is living within, and waiting and wanting to begin to live out His life through him. We had lunch on several occasions, and little by little he began to fully grasp the truth of that relationship. He was so excited to realize that all he needed to do was to tell the Lord he was available, totally at His disposal, moment by moment, and the Lord would begin His work as only He could. A few weeks went by and he, like Marshall, became disillusioned because it seemed that God wasn't doing anything; anything that Carl could see, at least. I had to remind him that what God does is His business.

When God chooses to visibly demonstrate His life through you to another, that is also His business. The whole functioning aspect of that relationship is His business. Our business is to remain available, and we do that by simply telling Him, "Lord, I am available today and whatever You want to do, that's fine." Furthermore, "Lord, if You choose not to do anything from my perspective, that also is Your business, thank You anyway. You are still Lord and I thank You for Your peace and joy, and all that You want to be in me. Thank You!"

Once again, he saw the simplicity and just began to enjoy what the Lord had revealed to him. His joy and peace were just incredible!

One day while at his business, typography, the phone rang and he answered in his usual style, "Good morning, Carl Luebke."

The person calling said, "Oh, I must have the wrong number."

After making sure, Carl said, "Yes, you have the wrong number," and hung up. As soon as he had put the phone down he prayed, "Lord, that was it, that wasn't a wrong number. I goofed, but thank You anyway." He had no more finished with that conversation with the Lord, and the phone rang again.

Once again he said, "Good morning, Carl Luebke." The same party was on the line and began to apologize for having called the wrong number again.

Carl declared, "No problem, but I don't think it is the wrong number."

The person on the other end of the line replied, "Excuse me, is this so and so?"

Carl responded by saying, "No, it isn't."

The person said, "Then I have the wrong number."

Carl continued, "I know I am not the person you intentionally called and I know you think you have reached a wrong number, but I really think you connected with me for a different reason." He went on to tell the caller of his newfound faith in Christ, and the discovery of His indwelling presence, and in the process of that telephone call, Carl had led that person to Jesus Christ! He is the only person I have ever met or heard of that had a "wrong number" ministry. One cannot plan to have a "wrong number" ministry. Only God can do that!

On another day, the phone rang and he went through his normal procedure of answering it. Sure enough, wrong number. He quickly said to the person, "I think for the first time in your life you have reached the right number." In the process of the conversation, Carl asked, "Where do you go to church?"

She answered, "I go to the Catholic church."

Carl said, "Great, do you go to church on Sunday evenings?"

She replied, "No."

Carl proceeded to invite her to come to church. He further said, "I promise you, if you will come just one time, I will not bother to try and keep you coming, or try to get you to leave your church. I just want you to hear my pastor. I think he is terrific."

The lady answered, "I would be glad to come, but would it be possible for me to bring my sister with me?"

Carl responded, "Of course, we would be delighted to have both you and your sister."

The following Sunday evening two Roman Catholic nuns walked into the church dressed in full habit. In the weeks that followed there were six nuns that attended our church every Sunday evening. On one Sunday evening the priest came with them! After the service was over, we were in the lower auditorium for a little food and fellowship. The priest came up to me and said, "Are you Pastor Bob?"

I answered, "Yes."

He introduced himself to me and we shook hands. Then he said, "I don't understand all of this," and with that he looked out over several hundred people who were obviously happy and having a great time with each other. "What is this about?" he questioned.

"What do you mean?" I asked.

"Look at them, they all look happy."

"They are happy. That is one of the requirements of being a member of this church," I quipped. "They must sign a document saying that they will always try to look happy whether they are or not."

He asked, "Really?"

I said seriously, "No, that isn't the reason they look happy. They look happy because they are happy." I had the further joy of sharing with that priest that the root of joy and happiness is not the church, but Jesus.

His response, "Very interesting."

Whom do you suppose planned that whole sequence of events in Carl's life. One of our committees? Not a chance, only God could have done that, and He did.

The whole point of this is that it takes God to be God. It takes the Lord Jesus to be the Lord Jesus. I am inadequate to do His work, so are you. Only God can do the work of God. He has in the past and will in the future. He is not an "it." He is the One that brought all of life into existence. He is the One that has redeemed us by virtue of His death, burial, and resurrection, and at this moment is living in us in the person of His other self, the Holy Spirit. He's just waiting for us to allow Him the right to live His life out through us. Let Him!

You see, the Lord Jesus, just before He was crucified, gathered His disciples about Him and shared with them the most significant and relevant "truth" that they would ever hear. There is no evidence that any of them understood what He was talking about. That "truth"?

Let me paraphrase; Jesus said, "In a little while, I am going away, but I will not leave you forever. I will come back and as my Father lives *in* Me, I will live in you. At that day, you shall know that I live in my Father and you *in* Me and I *in* you" (John 14:20).

There was no response from any of them. Ever wonder why? Rather simple, I think, they had no idea what He was talking about. It was inconceivable to think that a real live person could die and somehow in a few days come back in another form and take up residence within them. It was beyond belief, totally beyond their realm of understanding, hence, no response.

We, as the church, have as little understanding about that tremendous statement as the disciples, and consequently our response is just as evident. When was the last time you heard anyone proclaim the incredible truth that the Lord Jesus died in order to give His life to you, and thereafter He will begin to live His life through you?

The fact is that we hear just the opposite. "The Christian life isn't Christ living His life through us. The Christian life is us, doing the best we can on the behalf of Jesus." Soon we make the discovery that it isn't just difficult to live the Christian life; *it is impossible*, and we give up in total failure.

When Marshall and Carl said, "It didn't work," they were right. "*It*" doesn't work. But we are not talking about an "*It*," we're talking about the Lord Jesus, resident *in* our lives. The same Lord Jesus that took up residency in the lives of the disciples is now living *in* us, ready to accomplish what He desires.

The trouble is, we are so stubborn and rebellious, clinging to all of our evangelical hangups with the declaration of little Joel, "These are mine!" We never get around to discover the thrilling reality of His indwelling, much less the exciting demonstration of His life through us to others.

No, "it" won't work, but praise His name, *He will!* That's what this book is about, to discover the reality of His indwelling, and the demonstration of that reality through our lives.

Who Wants to Be a Butler?

I grew up hearing about "serving the Lord." We would sing, "I am happy in the service of the King," and as I looked about, I didn't see very many that looked happy, much less were happy. When the annual business meeting was in session, I was absolutely certain that no one was happy. It looked like just the opposite.

The following Sunday the rhetoric would continue. I, for one, was not interested in being an evangelical "butler." If I was going to serve anyone I would serve my self-interests first and if there was any time left, well, then maybe I might serve Him as was called in the church, the youth group, or maybe even in cleaning the church. I really didn't have a choice as to whether or not I would serve in that capacity, my mother donated my time. It wasn't a happy time "serving the Lord." I still hear the phrase "serving the Lord," and those who use it don't impress me as being overjoyed in the process.

There are those of us who are in "full-time service," as opposed to the majority of Christians who are not in "full-time service." The largest segment of Christian society are "laymen." They're just a cut or two under those who are in "full-time service." Mind you, it is great having those "laymen" who can't be in "full-time service." They make up that great contingent of people who "If you can't go, at least you can give." In addition to that, "If you can't go or give, at least you can pray."

That isn't a biblical system of defining "service," of course. If we were interested in a biblical definition of service we might see something different. For example, in John's gospel, chapter 12, the Lord Jesus said to those gathered around Him (verse 26), "If any man serve me, let him follow me."

Can you imagine being in that meeting and hearing Jesus say that? Perhaps we can even imagine being among the disciples, sitting there, looking at them. There is Peter, John, Matthew, Judas, and all the rest. They were so important. Others looked at them with envy, disgust, even desire to be one of "them." Then we hear Jesus say, "If *any* man serve me." *Any* man? That includes me, I think to myself. Yes, I want to serve Him, I do want to be part of His party. Yes! Yes! Yes! What did He say?

His words ring in my ears, "Follow Me."

If then I have decided to serve Him I would follow His instructions and "Follow Him." When He rose to leave, I would follow. Oh, not too close. I am not deserving to be too close, just close enough so that I don't lose track of Him. But where was He going?

If we are going to follow someone would it not be a good idea to find out where they are going before we follow? Sounds good to me. Where was He going? As He left that scene, He would make His way down a path or road, talking to people as He went. Perhaps He'd stop and have a drink of water along the way, or say a few words to those that were following close by. I follow.

The next day I continue to follow Him, and the next, and the next. My determination is to follow Him wherever He went, but where was He going? Ultimately, He was going to the cross to be crucified. That is just the point He was making. Not simply to get people to follow Him around that present moment to just be involved in a little "chit chat," although that would have been great. He wanted to find people who were prepared to follow Him to the cross and discover what it meant to be "crucified with

Him." We can only follow Christ to the point that it leads us to the cross. Not just to watch Him die and feel sympathy for Him, weeping and wailing over His suffering, but to join Him on the cross and die with Him.

After preaching about this, a lieutenant colonel in the air force came to me and asked, "What is the alternative to dying with Christ?"

I answered, "Well, let's find out what Jesus said." I turned to John 12:24, "Except a corn of wheat fall into the ground and die," and here is the alternative, "it abideth alone."

He responded, "That isn't much of an alternative."

"I didn't write it, I just read it. Jesus said it, not me." With that he turned and walked away.

The following year at the same conference he came rushing up to me, put his arms around me with a huge embrace and declared, "I've discovered what it is to die and for the first time in my Christian life I am now living!"

The songwriters have done us, the Christian public, an incredible disservice by writing hymns, choruses and songs about the need for us to "follow Him." We never catch up to Him. We just follow like little puppies ever trying to get closer to Him, but never being able to arrive at a closeness that is adequate.

The fact is that He didn't die in order for us to get closer to Him. He has no desire for us to follow at a distance; no desire to hold our hand. He didn't die for us in order that we might become some sort of evangelical "butler" in an attempt to satisfy all His needs. He didn't die for that. He died *for* us in order to give His life *to* us that He might indwell us, live *in* us. Why? So that He might live His life out through us. It is called a "relationship." A relationship of His indwelling, a personal relationship. Not just a factual relationship, but a functioning relationship.

When the Apostle Paul met the Lord Jesus on the road to Damascus it indeed was a personal encounter. He states in Galatians 2:20, "I am crucified with Christ; nevertheless I live, yet not I, but Christ liveth in me."

41

For years, that was one of my favorite verses, but for the life of me, I couldn't figure out the meaning and the effect it would have on my life. It was just another one of those verses that sounded great and spiritual. I didn't have a clue as to what it meant, much less what it said or how it worked in life.

To "follow Christ" will eventually take us to the cross, not for the purpose of standing around and looking at Jesus hanging on the cross; but rather to discover what it means to die with Him in order for Him to live His life in us and through us.

We sing hymns that depict Jesus hanging on the cross and we're standing nearby watching Him die. He didn't die for the purpose of His believers gathering at the foot of the cross to watch Him die. One of the most famous of all hymns, "The Old Rugged Cross," says, "So I'll cling to the old rugged cross." It is the Christian's favorite.

In a church I served as an interim pastor, I was engaged in conversation with one of the elders regarding this hymn. He took exception to some of the things I had said about it. He said, " 'The Old Rugged Cross' is my favorite hymn."

I questioned, "Why?"

He replied, "I just like it. I really cling to the cross as it says in the chorus."

My response to him was, "If you are going to cling to the cross as the hymn suggests, what in the world do you need Jesus for?" The question astounded him.

He sat silent for a moment, and finally said quietly, "I have never thought about that."

We sing songs and choruses without ever giving any thought as to the truth of the words. As long as the music has a "neat" little tune, we sing, it doesn't matter if it is true or not.

If you are going to serve Jesus, your service will take you to the cross where you discover how to die in order to discover how to live. Who wants to die? Not many.

The current thrust in the church is not to die, but rather to take control of your life. Seize the opportunity and fight the devil, in Jesus' name. Take authority over the devil, in Jesus' name, and cast out whatever demons and devils that happen to be around. So many demons and devils have been cast out through TV and radio I can't believe that there are any left to be cast out! That is, if the system and activity really work. While so many are taking authority over the devil and casting out every demon of sickness, there are others languishing in the reality of their illnesses, unable to find a way out. All the while, the people casting out the demons and devils of sickness continue to wear their glasses and hearing aids, and go on raising money for their ministries. This is dumbfounding!

The religious TV programs' plea to the listening audience is to give money under the premise that God will return it a hundredfold. Why don't the preachers and promoters just quietly decide to trust God for their needs just as they tell everyone else to do? Oh, I know, they don't want the audience to miss the blessing, yeah right! What is amazing to me is that the crowds continue to go bonkers upon hearing all of the above and respond with more and more money.

However, just let someone suggest going to the cross and die so He can live through them and there is little, if any, interest. Jesus said in John 15, "I am the vine. You are the branches." It doesn't take a rocket scientist to know that branches don't do much, they don't produce anything. They just bear what the vine produces. Branches have no authority, or status other than that of a branch. They have no effectiveness except as they remain available to the vine so that the vine can flow its resources through the branch. A branch is nothing more than a vehicle through which the vine can accomplish what it pleases: fruition. That isn't much, but that is real service!

Well, how does that work? To die means to come to that point in your life as a Christian when you know you are totally inadequate to live the Christian life. After a life of trying and effort on God's behalf and the overwhelming effects of failure and guilt, we have little to show for our effort except a life of total bankruptcy and barrenness.

Having spent a lot of my life in little Joel's attitude, "These are mine," I have come to the conclusion that there must be more to the Christian life than doing the best you can for Jesus. There has to be more to it than serving Jesus to the best of your ability.

Now I am prepared to give up and let Him take over. That point of utter desperation, total frustration with the ups and downs, the questioning, the depression, being utterly destitute of anything that resembles God in my life. I was absolutely and thoroughly disappointed and disgusted with God. I have spent innumerable hours praying and asking God to do what I want Him to do on my behalf and nothing happens. He not only doesn't answer, but the heavens are as brass. Enough is enough!

I remember that moment as though it were yesterday. I went through many months and years of attempting to be "happy in the service of the King." A huge problem in the process was the discovery that other "servants of the King" were not too happy and they let me know it. They were called "church members." These were church members who could reel off all the evangelical clichés and would just as quickly stab a brother in the back as to look at him, just because the other brother did not agree with him on some issue. If you don't believe it, check out the annual business meeting of the church. These same self-righteous "brothers" had all the answers to the problems.

I must admit that my solution to many of the problems of the church was to hope and pray that those people with those huge problems would finally leave and go to the Methodist church, any church but ours! After all, we wanted to keep our church "pure." Incredible! Oh, by the way, if you ever find a "pure" church, don't join it because you will certainly mess it up.

In my desire to serve Jesus to the best of my ability, I took on a new project; a "soul winners" course. I was not to be a student, I was the instructor. I devised a program in which several couples of my church would meet every Tuesday evening for two hours to discuss and learn how to be a "soul winner." This course went on for 26 weeks. I thought, "Now we are ready to go into the community and witness for the Lord." I announced to the class, "Next week we will meet at the church for the purpose of going into the community to witness. I have a number of people for each of us to see. I have their names and addresses. We will meet for a time of prayer, asking God's blessing on us as we go, and then we will go."

The following Tuesday I thought during the day, "We have reached a momentous time in our lives and in our church, this is it!" I went to the church early and waited eagerly for everyone to come. One person came, one person, other than my wife and myself. I was totally devastated. I had spent 26 solid weeks in preparation and one person came.

In the process of those weeks someone gave me a book on "revival." I read it with great interest. A part of the book was devoted to the subject of prayer. I was challenged by a question the writer asked, "Have you ever spent all night in prayer for those whom you want to come to Christ?" I had to admit that I had never done such a thing. I was further challenged to do so. Deep in my heart there was a desire to accomplish great things for God. If it took all night in prayer, so be it.

I set a particular night as my target night for prayer. I decided that I would not start my night of prayer until 11 P.M. (the night wouldn't be so long). I arrived at my study at 11 P.M. armed with a pot of coffee to help me stay awake. I started by praying for my immediate family, a process that was expressed essentially by asking God to bless my wife and my children. I asked that they might be kept in good health and to give them guidance, etc. When I looked at my watch, only 20 minutes had passed. If I was going to pray until 7 A.M. I still had seven hours and 40 minutes to go. I was already exhausted, however, I persevered.

I next put the church member directory in front of me and proceeded to pray for them in the same manner. When I opened my eyes, another 20 minutes or so had passed. I stopped for a cup of coffee. I continued by placing the telephone directory of our little town in front of me and began going through it as though I knew everyone in it. I explained to God that He knew all these people, and in all earnestness and dedication to the Lord Jesus, spent the next couple of hours going through it pleading with God to save them. Then came the yellow pages. I prayed for all the businesses. Some of them later went bankrupt. I don't know if my praying had anything to do with that or not.

Now it is 1:30 in the morning and I am exhausted, but I must continue. I walked to the local park a few blocks away and knelt at a park bench. For several hours I poured out my heart in massive sobbing and tears, to the point of total exhaustion.

As I watched the sun start its rise in the east, the satisfaction in my heart was overwhelming. I did it! Greater than that was the emotional high that I attained. There was a sense of spirituality that I had never sensed before.

Alas, as I arrived home to my family just getting up, they were unimpressed. They didn't even know I was gone nor why my eyes were so red, and looking like I had been up all night...I had been.

I went to bed and slept for a couple of hours and upon awakening, the sense of failure, bankruptcy and guilt just overwhelmed me. There is no way that I can adequately describe it. However, that night, I did it again. In fact, for a solid month I did it every night, all night long, and nothing happened, except that I became more frustrated and exhausted. My conclusion to the whole exercise? *It doesn't work!* Indeed *it* doesn't. *God does*, but I didn't know that.

How could I possibly choose that song to sing next week for the morning worship hour, "I'm Happy in the Service of the King"? Not a chance in this world that we will sing that song, I thought. At that moment, I didn't know what the song would be, but it certainly wouldn't be that one!

My heart cried with nearly a primal scream, "Oh, God, where are You? What is the Christian life about? Oh, God! Oh, God!" My heart was nearly broken with failure and grief to say nothing of the guilt.

Nevertheless, Sunday is just around the corner and I must get ready to preach. I must get it together and be able to tell everyone who comes that, "It is such a deep joy to be a Christian and wouldn't you like to become one?" Once again, I was busy, not happy, but busy in the service of the King. Am I the only person with this kind of problem, I thought? I don't think so, as a matter of fact, I know so.

How often have we been reminded that the Bible says we are to be witnesses for Christ? Being reminded, we probably haven't been the witness that we should be. We probably haven't prayed for the missionaries as much as we should. We surely haven't given as much as we should. The pressure is on to *perform*. To be some outstanding "butler" for Christ. To outperform the other brothers in church.

The fact is, the Bible doesn't say that we have to be witnesses. Acts 1:8 is where this misnomer comes from. It actually says that "We *shall* be witnesses," not have to be, "*shall* be." "What's the difference?" you say.

Jesus said, "We shall be witnesses," because He knew and had said to the disciples, several times, that shortly after His ascension, He would come back and take up His life within them in order to live His life through them. He knew full well that not one person present would be capable of living His life for Him. He also knew that He was capable of living His own life through them, if only they would let Him.

Read on in the book of Acts and you see a definitive description of the Lord Jesus being active through them. Their lives were not their own, they had been bought with the price of His death. Because the Father resurrected Him from the grave He is now alive and would soon come and live in them. He knew this, the disciples would soon know as well.

This is why the book of Acts begins by saying in verse one, "The former treatise have I made, O Theophilus, of all that Jesus began both to do and teach." The book of Acts is not the acts of the apostles, but rather the acts of the Lord Jesus *through* the apostles. They were just the branches of which He said, "He was the vine."

The apostles were not performing *for* the Lord Jesus. They were not giving it their best shot. They were not doing the best they could for Jesus. They were the available vehicle *in* which He lived, and through which He was demonstrating His life to all that came in contact. They were not performing butlers, but praising believers, praising Him for all that He was doing in and through them!

There is no record of them, at any time, sitting down and trying to decide what to do next for the Lord. They were just available to Him and weren't the slightest bit surprised at what happened next.

That same Lord Jesus is living *in* you, if you have received Him. He is not the slightest bit interested in what you can do for Him because He knows that if you attempt to do something on His behalf, you will fail. As a result of your failure there will be guilt and grief, so why bother?

Why not just tell Him you are available for whatever He might want to do with you, in you, and through you...hang the consequences! Step out by faith and in the language of faith say: "Thank You, Lord Jesus, for living in me. My life is totally at Your disposal for whatever You might want to do with me." Begin to enjoy the unlimited reality of His indwelling life. For the first time in your life you will discover the liberating reality of the "Christ life" rather than being beaten down with guilt and despair at having failed Him. Liberation and life!

Now, What Do I Do?

That's a great question. It's one thing to discover that we are inadequate for the task of living the Christian life, that we are totally burnt out, frustrated, inept, and depressed with the whole relationship. We're completely disappointed with God because He didn't come down and visually, physically do something. Not just "something," but the thing that I proposed for Him to do. Screaming to high heaven, "God, where are You? Why don't You do something? Why don't You answer me? *Why? Why? Why?*"

It's one thing to spiritually collapse in His presence, to be devastated by His silence and inactivity, and quite another to discover, "What to do about it."

Well, what do you do? One thing you don't do is get caught up in the "Oh, me, oh, my" syndrome and stay there for the rest of your life. Some have done that, living in retrospection, sorry for all the failures, suffering massive guilt and there be "stuck." Don't get stuck in that muck. Go on to realize that He has never expected any more from you than failure.

When the Lord Jesus began to share with His disciples the fact that He would be leaving in a while, John 13:33 tells us, "Little children, yet a little while I am with you. You shall seek me;

and as I said unto the Jews, whither I go, ye cannot come; so now I say to you." Then in verse 36, Peter speaks. Well, wouldn't you know it would be Peter, who "said"? Have you ever noticed in the gospels how many times it says, "And Peter answered and said," or words to that effect? Have you ever noticed how few times Peter was ever asked anything? Peter operated under the principle, "When in doubt, talk."

On the mount of Transfiguration, the Lord Jesus took Peter, James and John up into a high mountain, recorded in Mark 9. Verse 4 reveals that Elijah and Moses appeared and guess who spoke up? Peter, of course, but notice what he said, "Master, it is good for us to be here, and let us make three tabernacles; one for You, one for Moses, and one for Elijah. For he did not really know what to say, for they were in a violent fright, aghast with dread." Peter would have made a great pastor. When in doubt, build something.

Peter responds in John 13, "Where are you going?"

Jesus said very kindly and patiently, "Where I'm going, you cannot follow me now, but you will follow me afterwards."

Peter answers defiantly, defensively, "Lord, why can't I follow you now? I will lay down my life for you."

Jesus' response was devastating. Verse 38, "Will you lay down your life for me, Peter? The day will not dawn before you will have denied me three times."

To put this in perspective, one has to imagine being in church and it is time for the invitation and I am overcome with conviction, as a Christian. I haven't been the Christian I should have been. I have failed the Lord on numerous occasions. I have just been reminded of that, and now the invitation to "come forward," re-commit myself to the Lord with the resolve that, "from now on, I am going to be different, with the Lord's help." So, I go forward, broken, to meet the pastor.

When he sees me coming, he whispers in my ear, "Why are you coming forward?"

As simply as I know how, through the sobbing and grief of my failure and guilt I admit to him that I haven't been all that I should be. I just want the church to know that I am here to recommit myself to Jesus in the hope that from now on, I am going to be different.

He listens intently, and I notice a little chuckle emerging from his throat. Confused, I continue and finish my statement to him, in a whisper.

When I am finished, he turns to the congregation and shares with them what I had just told him in private, and then says to the congregation, "We all know Bob, he has come forward before. We know what a phony he is, what a failure, and hypocrite he is."

With each declaration, he raises his voice, then says to me still standing in front of the congregation, "You have always been a failure and a phony. You always will be a phony and a failure of the worst sort. We all know you for what you are. You will never be any different, now go back to your seat and be quiet."

What do you suppose my response would be in that situation? What would you think if it happened to you? That is exactly what happened to Peter. Publicly exposed for his inability to live out his commitment to Christ; totally humiliated in front of his fellow disciples. He was prepared to shrink away into the shadows and get lost.

Before he could do that, Jesus furthers the conversation in the next verse, chapter 14, verse one. Unfortunately, there is a chapter division at that point. There should not have been, for the context continues, "Let not your heart be troubled."

Guess whose heart was troubled? Troubled isn't the word for it. Peter was devastated. He looked around at the other disciples. Of course, they knew him for the loud mouth that he was, and now fully exposed for the phony that everyone already knew him to be.

The Lord Jesus continued speaking not only to Peter, but to all the disciples, in that exchange Philip spoke of in verse 8, quoting from the King James translation, "Shew us the Father, and it sufficeth us." Get your Bible, and read it for yourself as Jesus continued, "Have I been so long time with you, and yet hast thou not known me, Philip? he that hath seen me hath seen the Father;

51

and how sayest thou then, Shew us the Father?" Read very carefully, "Believest thou not that I am in the Father, and the Father in me? the words that I speak unto you I speak not of myself: but the Father that dwelleth in me, he doeth the works."

In that short sentence, the Lord Jesus is revealing for the first time in His life what His relationship to the Father was and is. He said, "My Father is in me and I am in my Father. The works that I do are not mine, they're His. The words that I speak are not mine, they're His."

In essence He said, "My Father lives *in* Me and I live in my Father. As I remain totally available to my Father living *in* Me, He is prepared to live through Me all that He desires. I live in this relationship 24 hours a day seven days a week. This is my relationship to and *in* my Father."

The response from the disciples? There was none. None! Why? Simply because they hadn't the foggiest notion of what He was talking about. He knew they didn't know, for later on in verse 20 he says, "At that day." Which day? The day of the coming of the Holy Spirit at Pentecost, Acts 2. "At that day, you will know that I am in my Father and you in Me and I in you." Their response? Once again, *nothing*.

What was He saying in all of this? He was sharing with them the incredible relationship that He had with and in His Father. One day, they would have the same relationship to Him and *in* Him as He had in His Father. Their response? *None*. They didn't understand what He was talking about. Soon they would, and did at the day of Pentecost when He came back as He said He would in the person of His other self, the Holy Spirit, took up residence upon them and *within* them, never to be the same.

This is one of the most, if not *the* most, historic and momentous time in scripture, apart from the crucifixion and resurrection of Jesus. The relationship between God and man changes, never to be the same again. It changes from simply God being *with* us to God being *in* us. Is there any difference between the two relationships? Of course, it is like the difference between day and night. The disciples had been with the Lord Jesus for three solid years, and it didn't make a shekel's worth of difference in their lives. Peter, as the Lord predicted, denied Him. Judas betrayed Him. All of them forsook Him and fled from Him as He hung upon the cross. Great, faithful, and mighty disciples, wouldn't you say? But they were no different than any Christian alive now or since that day.

Why do you suppose Jesus predicted Peter's denial? The answer is simply that He knew the stuff of which Peter was made. What kind of stuff was that? The Scripture is quite clear on that subject. Jeremiah 17:9 says, "The heart is deceitful above all things, and desperately wicked...." What is the heart? It certainly is not that organ in our chest that keeps us alive. No, the heart is that real you living inside your body.

As we are with people and talk with them on a daily basis, they think they are seeing us as well as listening to us. But they are wrong. They are not seeing *us*, all they are seeing is the house we live in. The real me and the real you is on the inside, and very rarely do we let anyone see the real us.

This house we live in is marvelous. It comes with windows, called eyes. We can see out, but others cannot see in. We like that arrangement for we keep concealed the real you and the real me, or at least we attempt to. However, the Scripture that reveals the stuff of which Peter was made is the same Scripture that reveals the stuff of which we are made. We, too, are in that same category of the "heart that is deceitful and desperately wicked."

Have you ever noticed that when our children are born we do not have to send them to school to teach them to be selfish. Where do they get that bent? Naturally, from their mother and their father. It is built in.

One can think of all the other negative traits that do not have to be taught to us. It is just the natural thing to do. However, have you noticed that when we become Christians, we no longer have that selfish tendency? *Not a chance!* What makes the Christian selfish? The same thing that makes the little child selfish. Just because you become a Christian does not mean that all these natural traits have disappeared, even a little bit. No! They are just as strong today in the life of a believer as they are in the life of an unbeliever. The unbeliever, becoming agitated or angered, will often spit out a number of expletives. When the believer becomes agitated or angered, the expletives have changed.

Instead of calling someone something gross, we have "evangelized" our profanity and now call that stupid driver in front of us, taking his time, getting in our way, impeding our progress of getting where we want to go... an "idiot," "jerk," or "dingbat," hollering at him, "Get out of my way! Move it! If the light gets any greener it will grow." "Where in the world did he get his driver's license, from a Wheaties box?"

On and on it goes. The attitude of the unbeliever and believer alike are the same: anger, agitation, disgust, etc. We have just cleaned up our vocabulary act. Big deal. The Christian life is certainly a lot more than just cleaning up your vocabulary.

To predict Peter's failure was a very simple thing for Jesus to do. Knowing what we know now, we could have predicted it. Obviously, we can also predict our failure. Having been made of the "same stuff," it is absolutely predictable that we will fail also, and we do.

When did you last fail the Lord? You don't have to think too far in the past. Have you ever failed the Lord on the Lord's day? Naturally, I can't imagine anyone failing the Lord on the Lord's day, of all days. Is it possible to "not fail" that one day of the week? I think not.

Why did you fail? Was it a premeditated act? Did you decide when you got out of bed that, "Today would be a good day to fail the Lord, I guess I will do that"? Of course not, to fail Him is all that we are qualified to do. It is about the only talent we have, and we are good at it. We even fail Him on Easter Sunday, that great time of resurrection celebration. Why? It is all you can do by virtue of the stuff of which you are made, it is a helpless and hopeless situation.

Someone says, "Well, we don't have to fail. We can overcome our failure, we can be what we ought to be." Really? Do you know anyone that has succeeded? I don't. Why do we fail when that is the last thing we want to do? It's a simple principle: like produces like. If you plant wheat, chances are you will harvest wheat. No, it is not "chances are," it is an absolute fact, plant wheat, harvest wheat. You don't have to be some amazing prophet to predict that. It is simply a fact.

But let's say the farmer speaks to his many bags of seed in a loud, authoritative voice, "Listen up wheat. I do not have any seed oats to plant this year, can't afford to buy it. So listen, I want you to produce oats. I realize that it is going to be tough, but you can do it. All you need to do is put your mind to it. It is oats I want this year, so do the best you can."

The little kernels of wheat listened incredulously and got together after the farmer went back to the house. They said, after much discussion, "If the man wants oats, then oats it is. It is up to us to fulfill the desires and wishes of this man. He is our master and we will obey."

After the wheat had been planted, you could go by the field, listening very carefully you could hear the little kernels giving it their best shot. Try as they may, when at last they died and the new life came up out of the ground, alas, it was wheat. Disappointed with their efforts, they had failed and failed miserably. They hung their heads in depression and defeat, total failures. Really? Total failures? I think not. They had produced what they were qualified to produce: wheat. Why should they hang their heads in depression and defeat? It was all they could do.

Listen, Christian friend of mine. If you are in the throes of depression and defeat because you have failed the Lord, it is needless. You are only doing and performing what you are qualified to do: fail. You are good at it. We have the proof. The simple conclusion is that the Christian life is not difficult, it is impossible. There is only *One* who cannot fail and that is the Lord Jesus. He died for you in order to give His life to you, to live and do in, and through you what you cannot do.

For 33 years Jesus had a body. Why? He had a body to use to get around in. By virtue of His birth, life, death, and resurrection, He has purchased a new body: you and me. We are called the body of Christ. As He used His earthly body to get around in, He now uses us, His purchased body, the body of Christ, to get around in. All He is looking for is a few people that will allow Him to do what He planned.

As He lived in the Father, we now live in Him. As the Father lived in Him, He now lives in us. The purpose in both relationships is exactly the same. His was to allow the Father to live, speak, and demonstrate His life and purpose through Jesus. Jesus' purpose for living in us, is to live through us. As the Father lived through Him, now He wants to live through us. He knows full well, without a doubt, that we cannot live His life for Him. He never expected us to even try. Rather, He has placed at our disposal the joy of trusting Him to do in and through us what He knows we cannot do. It is called *trust*, not try. So what do I do? Simple, trust Him. Remember, the language of trust is, *thank You!*

I had the joy of meeting Dr. Conrad Milne (see foreword), at a Bible Conference just north of Toronto, Ontario. Dr. Milne is presently a retired professor of New Mexico State University, Las Cruces, New Mexico. He was the camp conference athletic director.

In the process of the week, Connie began to discover the truth that I have been writing about. Some time later, he called me and asked where I was going to be the third week of March of that year. I looked at my diary and said, "I am going to be in Houston, Texas."

He responded by saying, "That's amazing, I am going to be in Houston the exact same week. Would it be possible for us to get together?" I reassured him that it would not only be possible, but that I would look forward to seeing him.

We met in Houston and he told me the story of his father who was not a Christian. He related how he had really tried to witness to him, and on some occasions had put the pressure on him to accept Christ. His dad had rejected all that Connie had tried to convince him as the truth. Connie was discouraged and didn't know what to do. I reminded him that not only could he not do it, but that it was impossible. In our discussion, he hung his head with tears running down his face, a total failure.

I finally broke the silence and said, "Connie, do you remember that Jesus Christ lives in you."

He answered, "Yes."

I continued, "He wants your dad to come to Him more than you do. *He* died for him. All He is waiting for you to do is to tell Him you are available to Him and launch out in faith, in the language of faith and say, 'Thank You, Lord Jesus, for what and how You are going to deal with my dad.'" He instantly saw the simplicity.

I further advised Connie, "When you get home, don't say anything more to your dad on the subject. When you go into his house, greet him, embrace him, and tell him you love him and let it go at that."

Connie called me a short time later, and told me this story, "I was thoroughly convinced the Lord Jesus was living within me. I was further convinced that He was adequate to meet the need of my dad's heart and life. I knew that there was nothing that I could do. I continued to pursue the 'availability...attitude,' telling Him that I was totally available, not only generally to Him, but in particular as it related to my dad.

"One night, the Lord laid my dad so heavily upon my heart, I felt constrained to drive the 80 miles from London to Guelph...just to see my dad. I just told Mary, 'I have to go. Bye.'

"It was a trip of incredible expectancy, without the normal pleading with God to 'Do something!' I simply said, 'Lord Jesus, You live *in* me, thank You very much. I live *in* You, and I am extremely grateful that You have allowed me the privilege of discovering this relationship. Thank You for what You are going to do through me tonight through this available vessel. Thank You!' I walked into their house, hugged them both and told each one that I loved them. I had the joy of talking with both my mom and dad. As it turned out, my mom had received Christ when she was a young girl. As I talked with my dad, it wasn't long before he broke down and began to cry. In a few minutes we were both kneeling in front of the chesterfield [couch] and I had the joy of leading my dad to the Lord Jesus!

"That was my greatest experience of 'being available,' and witnessed firsthand, the Lord Jesus witnessing through me. The return trip to London was 80 miles of rejoicing!"

Who do you think arranged all of that? It is amazing what God can do, it is almost like He knows what He is doing. Certainly, He does. He is just looking for some people through whom to have it happen.

I have had people say to me, "That may work for some people, but not for me. I don't have any talent or abilities. I am just a nobody." Did you know God is searching for those who would be available to Him? He seeks people who would respond, allowing Him to work within and through their lives. Second Chronicles 16:9 says, "The eyes of the Lord run to and fro throughout the whole earth, to shew himself strong in the behalf of them whose heart is perfect toward him...." A perfect heart is simply a person who has come to an end of himself, and has granted Him the right to do and be anything God wants to do and be.

It isn't that I have to somehow arrive at a point of usability. It isn't usability, it is availability. Why did God use that particular bush in the desert to speak through to Moses? Was that the only bush that had been to college and seminary? Was that the only bush that was qualified to be used, or had learned how to be effective for God? What nonsense! God used that bush because that was the bush that was available. It was simply that.

That is the most incredible principle I have ever discovered in the Word. The simplicity of availability. It follows that God is not interested in my ability, because my ability is total inability. His ability is total dependability. My responsibility is total availability.

So what do I do? I tell Him, "I am completely inadequate!" (I can hear Him say, "Oh, really?") "I give up!" (He says, "It's about time.") "I am going to trust You with my life. I place myself totally at Your disposal, totally available to You, to do exactly as You please. By the way, thank You, in advance, for what You are going to do!"

Can you think of anything better to do?

The Christian Life Isn't Difficult . . . It's Impossible!

The first time I heard that statement I nearly went into orbit. What in the world is he talking about, I quietly and angrily asked myself? How can that be, the Christian life impossible? As I thought it over, and it didn't take long, I had to admit that I for one, was a complete failure at living the Christian life.

That's what was so frustrating. The endless "trying to live for Jesus." The agony of trying to "witness for Jesus." Having heard from the very beginning of my Christian life that it was my responsibility to do all of that and more, I tried and failed miserably.

It all began to come into clear focus during the first five years of my ministry under the pressure of having to prepare so many new sermons each week. The frustration and depression was nearly intolerable. For me there wasn't any answer except to do as they say, "Keep on keeping on." What a ridiculous statement that is. That simply means stay in the rut doing the best you can. Eventually, you will see light at the end of the tunnel, and you do, a train heading straight for you! Thanks, but no thanks.

To face the reality that I was incapable of living the Christian life was on the one hand insulting. After all, hadn't I given it my best shot? Didn't I give my all? Indeed, I had...and failed. On the other hand, it was incredibly liberating.

To discover that I was inadequate was one thing. To admit it was quite another. I remember the day of that admission. Words are inadequate to describe all of the emotions that surged through me. I prayed, "Lord, You are right, I am inadequate. I've proved it over and over again by the way I've failed. You never expected anything more from me than failure. You never said that I could live Your life, the Christian life. On the contrary, there is every evidence in Scripture that tells me I cannot live the Christ life, and for all these years I have been living up to Your expectation of me. I cannot live the Christian life...because I am not Christ."

I discovered that it takes Christ to live the Christ life. A simple discovery that the root word of Christian is Christ; not Baptist, or Methodist, but Christ. Not any other denomination, but Christ.

Some get even more angry and irritated than I did at first. "Don't tell me that I can't live the Christian life. I have been living it for nearly 50 years." Really? Just ask his wife and children how successful he was and is.

Some go off to a conference or seminar to get a spiritual "shot" in the arm and come home all excited demonstrating their conviction with tears and admonition to others that they need to get closer to the Lord.

I was talking to someone the other day and she was telling me how her father went to a seminar and came home all excited. She went on to tell of what was happening in the home and finally ended her conversation by saying, "I think Dad needs to go off to another seminar." Whoopee for the seminar!

Why should anyone get irritated or angry at being told they can't live the Christian life when we know Someone who can? Now, that is exciting! In the midst of my failure and defeat I know somebody who can do what I can't do. What could be greater than that? The bigger problem is coming to the conclusion that failure and defeat is the norm and I'll just accept it as such, and be quite satisfied with the status quo.

Dr. Lewis Bock was a brilliant physician and committed Christian. I loved to hear him teach a Sunday school class. Many times in the midst of his lesson he would pause and say, "As Paul says in

1 Timothy," and then would quote from memory several verses of that passage.

There was only one thing wrong, he was a failure at the Christian life, just like the rest of us. That was a source of incredible irritation to not only him, but his family. Eventually, he began to discover the *One* who was adequate, and made that liberating discovery that Jesus Christ was his life.

Before he went to be with the Lord in 1985, he had written several articles, one of which he entitled "The Status Quo." Keep in mind as you read the following, this was written by a man who was extremely intelligent, not only in his field as a physician, but nearly any subject you wanted to discuss. He could come up with facts and figures, historic dates, etc. You name it, he could converse with you about it.

"The Status Quo"

"I'm so tired of mediocrity, Lord...
 Weary of the common place,
  Jaded by the customary,
 Of business as usual,
 Of life restrained,
  Shallow and muted.
Tired
Of preoccupation with trivia,
  Small talk and egomania,
  And knowledge falsely, so-called.
Tired
Of confusion called art,
  Noise called music,
  Of dysphonia praised.

"Tired
Of self-centered anarchy,
  Empty and deceptive,
  Vacuous and suspect,
  Embracing the usual
    As exceptional and normal;
    Herd mentality,
    Unquestioned acceptance
      Of what nature suggests,
      Undisciplined and self-
        indulgent...
      The 'everybody does it'
        Syndrome.
"Tired
Of great swelling words,
  Form without substance,
  Religion, lacking power,
    Profession and little more.

    Conformity without resistance,
    Life minus veracity,
    Suppositions without challenge.
      Approval before proof,
      Fizz instead of ebullience,
        Observation, not
          participation,
        Frustration plus
          nothingness.
        With nowhere to go!

"When You were here, Lord,
  You promised life abundant...
      Overflowing, pressed down,
      Shaken together and running over.

"You said, 'He that believes in me,
  As the Scripture has said,
  From him shall flow
  Living streams of water...'
        Out of internal reservoirs
        Alive and life-giving,
        Abundant, satisfying...His gift,
            God's Spirit within.

"Never let me affirm the status quo
  Embrace the mediocre,
  Accept the commonplace,
For this denies Your Presence,
  Makes me tell lies about You,
  And repudiates the purpose of Pentecost.
        Estranges me from my heritage,
            Shames the Son of God
            And denigrates His purposes
                For my world.

"So, Lord, I search my heart.
  In Your Presence
      I bare my soul.
  To know this mystery among the nations,
      My hope of glory now and forever....

"Christ *in* me...
  God's great secret!
Completely whole
Vibrantly alive, totally free!"

Lew had made that revolutionary discovery that Jesus Christ
had come not only to save him, but to be his life. Paul the apostle
has something to say about that in Colossians 3:3 from the Amplified translation, "For [as far as this world is concerned] you have
died, and your [new, real] life is hid with Christ in God."

Several factors leap out from that passage. First, the fact that there is a "new, real life." Not just a moment in time when I received Jesus into my life and for a while was thrilled, and felt like telling everybody about it. Not just for a period of time (relatively short) when I experienced a real joy and peace. Every Christian knows what this is about. Everyone who has ever come to the knowledge of Jesus Christ as Savior knows that first love and enthusiasm.

We also know what it is when that joy dissipates. Then the procedure is to go off to some conference or seminar and learn how to "share our faith," or "be spirit filled."

When we first came to Christ we didn't need anyone to teach us how to share our faith. We simply told other people what had happened. We didn't have all the answers. We didn't even know the questions.

If you have ever been in a church where people are regularly coming to Christ, not as a result of some high pressure evangelist or preacher, but coming to Christ as the legitimate result of Jesus Christ at work in and through the believers, there are always some Christians who are embarrassed at the new, fresh enthusiasm of the new convert. They unashamedly tell the new convert, "We have all had that first spurt of enthusiasm wanting to tell everybody with joy and a smile on our face, but you wait, it won't last. It will fade and you will become like us, just normal everyday Christians. So tone it down a bit, you are an embarrassment to us."

A new convert actually called me one day with the above scenario and said, "Pastor Bob, is it true that this won't last?"

My response was, "Well, that's what the Bible says. Remember what Jesus said, 'I've come that you might have life and that you might have it more abundantly...for about six months and then it will slowly but surely fade away.' "

She screamed through the telephone, "It does not say that!"

I said, "I know. His promise is His promise. It is true, and He can be trusted."

With that, she hung up the phone and there was no evidence of any fading in her life. She was an embarrassment to those who were defeated and discouraged and still holding up a good, so-called "Christian front." We're good at that.

The second factor is that new, real life has been "hidden." That is so strange to tell us about our new, real life, that He hid it, then proceeds to tell us where He hid it. I thought the purpose of hiding something was to keep others from finding whatever it was we hid. If our new, real life is hid, where do you suppose we are going to find it? I would presume that we will find that life precisely in the place where He hid it, in Christ. It's not hid in prayer, not in Bible study, or meditation. It's not in Scripture memory, or dedication, or in what people call praise and worship, but *in Christ*. It isn't that these other things aren't important, for they are. However, we won't find our new, real life in those things...only in Christ.

The word "hid" means to "cover or conceal properly." He has covered or concealed properly our new, real life. In Matthew 16:13, Jesus asked His disciples, "Whom do men say that I the Son of man am?"

They answered, "Some say that You are John the Baptist: some, Elias; and others, Jeremias, or one of the prophets."

He said in verse 15, "But whom do you say that I am?"

Wouldn't you know Peter answered, "Thou art the Christ, the Son of the living God"?

Jesus makes an incredible response in verse 17 and I paraphrase, "You are exactly right, Peter. For flesh and blood has not revealed this unto you, but my Father which is in heaven." The word "revealed" is an amazing word. It means,"to take off the cover." To reveal something is to take off the cover of something and allow someone to see what is underneath. Jesus hid our new, real life. He covered it, concealed it properly, and He is the only One that can take the cover off and allow us to see all the splendor and majesty of our new, real life! I can tell you about it, but I cannot take off the cover. I can preach and teach about it, but He is the only one that has the capacity to reveal it, or to take off the cover.

65

If you ever see or discover the reality of what has been hidden...your new, real life in Christ, you will never be the same. You can know intellectually and theologically the truth of His indwelling Presence, but never see and enter in to the truth of that new, real life found, not only *in* Jesus Christ, but by His indwelling.

I had a class years ago called "Christian ethics." I received straight A's in the class, but did not have a clue as to what the professor was talking about. The class was about Christ living in the believer. I knew all the answers relating to the subject but didn't *know*. He had not yet taken the cover off and allowed me to see the reality of that new, real life which is Christ in you, the hope of glory (Colossians 1:27).

People say to me who also knew my instructor, Ethel Wilcox, "Oh, you took the course taught by Ethel Wilcox, didn't you?"

My response is always, "Yes, I did, but I didn't discover from Ethel Wilcox. She tried desperately to teach us, because the message of His indwelling was a burning fire in her soul. However, it took Jesus to take off the cover and allow me to see the reality of my new, real life."

As Jesus said to Peter, "...Flesh and blood hath not revealed it unto thee, but my Father which is in heaven" (Matthew 16:17). It takes God to reveal God. It takes Jesus to reveal Jesus. He is the only one capable of taking off the cover.

If you are saying to yourself, "I know that Jesus is alive, and living in me. I learned that at Bible school. I was taught that at seminary." If you have approached the subject as an intellectual, spiritual concept that can be learned by our ability, then you have missed the point. You have missed the reality of discovering your new, real life. For if the Lord Jesus ever takes the cover off for you personally, and allows you to look and see the reality of His indwelling presence, you will never be the same!

I made that statement at an annual conference of Christian leaders, and a few months later one of them wrote to me and reminded me of what I had said. He went on to say that he began to rethink the whole principle of Christ living within the believer and all of a sudden it dawned on him...Jesus is actually alive and living *in* me!

He said, "I have known that for several years, but I didn't *know* it. Now I know, He is alive and living *in* me." His next statement was, "When can you come and lecture?" I have been going back every year since. I still cannot teach others and bring them into the reality of their new, real life. I can tell them, and I do, but only He, the Lord Jesus, has the capacity to "take off the cover."

Indeed, the Christian life isn't difficult...it is impossible! The more quickly we recognize and acknowledge that is true, the sooner we will begin to discover our new, real life in Christ Jesus.

Does It Matter . . . What Jesus Said?

The indwelling Lord Jesus Christ is the One who comes to inhabit our bodies the moment we invite Him to come in. You would be amazed at the various responses I receive from people as I have traveled over the face of this earth. The continual response is, "It's just a matter of semantics, just a matter of words. You say it one way, someone else says it in other words. It's all the same." Really?

Does it matter what Jesus said, or is the songwriter the final authority of truth? For you see, the songwriter has for years, and still does, dominate the theology of what people believe about Christ.

It doesn't seem to matter what the Word of God says, or what Jesus said. It seems to be up to the songwriter to write songs about God and Jesus. Those songs must rhyme, it doesn't matter if it's the truth or not; just so the words have a nice sound. Forget the truth...it doesn't matter, or does it?

I am of the opinion that it does matter. It was the Lord Jesus who said on many occasions that He was not only going to die, but that He would come back in the person of His other self, the Holy Spirit, and take up residence *within* the believer.

He said to the woman at the well in John 4:14, "...The water that I shall give him shall be *in* him a well of water springing up into everlasting life."

Doesn't it matter what He said? Is it the truth? Or is it just a partial truth that can be eliminated or watered down by words that refer to Him being by our side, or in front of us, that we can follow Him? Is what He said the truth?

He said, "I'll be *in* you." He's not beside you, not around you, in front, or behind you. He's not over or under you, but *in* you. If He said, "I'll be *in* you," would it be too much to presume that that is what He meant? I think not.

The Christian community a few years ago was caught up in the song, "Just a Closer Walk With Thee." We took it hook, line, and sinker, as gospel. It is not gospel. He did not come as a wee babe in Bethlehem to live His life of 33 years to be culminated by His death, burial, and resurrection for the purpose of us somehow, through unknown efforts of piety and works, make it possible to "get closer" to Him. How close can you get when you are *in* Him? Another old hymn of the faith says,

"Marvelous grace of our loving Lord,

Grace that exceeds our sin and our guilt;

Yonder on Calvary's mount outpoured;

There where the blood of the Lamb was spilt."

May I be so bold as to say the blood of the Lamb was not "spilt" at the cross. Spilling denotes an accident, and His death on the cross was no accident. He gave His life voluntarily, graciously, and completely for you and me. We dare say that His blood was shed due to an accident of spilling? Never!

Naturally, the songwriter needed a word that rhymes with "guilt" and the word "spilt" certainly does rhyme. What an incredible disservice to the Christian to tell us that His death was an accident of spilling! We Christians say nothing about it. We sing it as though it were gospel, and we have sung it for so long we have come to the conclusion it must be true. Or else we are just singing words and have no idea what they mean, and don't care to either think about it much less investigate the truth.

70

Doesn't it matter what Jesus said? I would venture to say that upwards of 90 percent of hymns, songs, and choruses refer to an external Jesus. An external Jesus sent to be with us, beside us to help us on with our earthly journey. We, the church, sing them as though they were true.

Someone said recently from the pulpit, "Jesus has promised to take us by the hand and lead us in the way." What utter nonsense! The church responded with a quiet "Amen."

Another church was singing about "manna." The conclusion of the song was that there is "Holy manna all around." Holy manna? Do we have any idea what the manna was for? We find the story in the book of Exodus. Israel had just come out of Egypt by virtue of the shed blood of an innocent lamb. A wonderful picture of the Lord Jesus, Lamb of God, slain before the foundation of the world. They came to the Red Sea and murmured and complained to Moses and God about their situation, and the Lord miraculously led them through the Red Sea, on dry ground.

The liberal theologian scoffs at such a concept, and tries to explain it away by saying that at that point in time, there was only about six inches of water involved so it would have been no problem for them to cross. The Scripture continues by saying that the Egyptian army was swallowed up by the water. A greater miracle, the Egyptian army drowning in six inches of water. Incredible!

The Israelites came through the Red Sea victorious, but it wasn't long before they were hungry. Once again, they found themselves in a state of grumbling and complaining, and the Lord sent them manna. Do you know what the word "manna" means? It means, "what is it?" It was given to them because of their constant grumbling and complaining. God's plan for them was the land of Canaan; the land that flowed with milk and honey. Because of their murmuring He gave them "what is it?" and for 40 years they ate "what is it?" Yet the songwriter talks about, "There is holy manna all around." Jesus did not die on a cross to provide "what is it?" for you as a Christian. He was crucified, buried, and raised from the dead in order for you to not only invite Him into your life, but to discover your new, real life in Christ

71

Jesus. He's the bread of life, the water of life, *life* in its fullest dimension.

My favorite little chorus in the days of my early ministry was, "He holds my hand, Jesus holds my hand." Major W. Ian Thomas, whom I had just met, reminded me that that chorus was much too external. I hadn't a clue what he meant, and I was offended that he should say such a thing about my little, lovely "plastic horse"! He was right! He had touched a very sensitive nerve in my life for which I have been and will be eternally grateful.

Maybe I have touched a sensitive nerve in your life, I hope and trust so. Enough so that you will begin to think, to consider the fact that this is not something I have dreamed up. This is not just another little emphasis, but the truth. This is what Jesus said to His disciples, "I am going to come and live *in* you," what a gift! Does it matter what Jesus said? Indeed it does.

The next time you hear a song that speaks of Him being beside you, or somewhere around you, just change the words quietly in your mind. Sing with a new note of praise in your heart and life that He lives within, rather than outside you.

There are heaps of people stuck in the Old Testament. Don't misunderstand, the Old Testament is important and as informative as it ever has been. However, keep in mind that the Old Testament is primarily the history of the Jewish nation, but more importantly, the prophetic revelation of the Lord Jesus, the Messiah. The Messiah would be born, live, crucified, and raised from the dead.

The relationship that God had with His people was always an external one, but for one or two instances when God stepped into a person. When the Lord Jesus commenced His earthly ministry it was with a view to His impending death, burial and ultimate resurrection. The specific purpose of His coming was for the indwelling of those whom He had redeemed. It was never with a view of continuing the external relationship of the past. Yet, we as the church are bombarded with so-called truth in songs and choruses that relate to us that Jesus is everywhere but *in* us.

Some choruses from the Old Testament talk about God being with us and around us, to help us. The Old Testament gave way to the Jesus of the New Testament who said, "I will come and live *in* you," and we ignore Him as though it is either not true or unimportant. It is true...unquestionably true.

However, the reason He comes to indwell us is in order to take control of us, and therein lies the problem. Our innate nature is such that, "No one is going to take control of me. No one is going to tell me what to do, I am in control of my life. I do as I please, and no one will change that, not even God. After all, *'these are mine!'* "

The apostle Paul spoke to this control issue. Ephesians 5:17 says, "Wherefore be ye not unwise, but understanding what the will of the Lord is." "Don't be unwise." In other words, don't be dumb about something, but understand. Understand what? What the will of the Lord is. What is His will? Verse 18, "And be not drunk with wine, wherein is excess; but be filled with the Spirit." We hear everyday on television and radio of the need to be filled with the Spirit. I have yet to hear anyone tell me what the word "filled" means. Would it be too much to expect, as a listener, when being challenged to "be filled with the Spirit," to ask what the word "filled" means? How can I be "filled" unless I know what the word means?

There is much discussion and preaching about this and from my vantage point, much confusion. There needn't be...the word "filled" means *control*. So when Paul says "to be filled with the Spirit," he means to be controlled by the Spirit.

There are four points to discover about being filled, or controlled by the Spirit:

1. It is a plurality. By that, it means that *every* believer is to be filled or controlled by the Spirit. This is not just for a few "super saints," but everyone. Every believer is to be filled, therefore controlled by the Spirit.
2. It is in the present tense. It should be translated as follows: "Be ye being filled with, controlled by the Holy Spirit, mo-

ment by moment." Not one massive, explosive, emotional once-and-for-all experience, but rather a moment by moment relationship in the Lord Jesus.

3. This filling or controlling is passive, which is to say "it is one acted upon." In other words, we cannot fill or control ourselves. That cuts right across our nature to be the best and first. The right to be in control of our lives is forever given to the One who bought us, and now lives in us to control us.

4. It is an imperative, a command. To be filled or controlled with the Spirit is not a suggestion by the Spirit, it is a command.

When the Lord Jesus comes into our lives the moment we receive Him, He comes in the person of His other self, the Holy Spirit to invade every aspect of our humanity for the specific purpose of totally controlling us. He allows us the right to retain the full capacity of our will, to either do as we please or to yield to His control. We have the privilege to yield to Him, moment by moment, thereby being filled with or controlled by Him, or we can stubbornly choose to do it our way. These rag dolls and plastic horses are mine, we can choose to do it, "Joel's way."

When we choose to make that choice to yield completely to Him, moment by moment, we have the privilege of being the vehicle through which He will live out His life, joy, and peace; sometimes in the midst of incredible strife and difficulty. That is what Paul called the "peace that passeth understanding." That is what it means to be called a branch, of which He is the Vine. He is in control!

74

So What?

I asked one day while preaching, "What do you do with the promises of God?"

A little lady answered, "I underline them in yellow." A rather interesting answer with which we all can identify. But really, what do you do with the promises of God other than underline them in yellow?

We used to sing, "Standing on the Promises of God." I had no idea what that meant. No one ever got around to telling me what it meant or what one does to "stand" on the promises, and I never asked. It seemed to me that most people were "sitting on the premises," rather than "standing on the promises."

As a matter of fact, the "Christian life," or what was presented as the Christian life, was mostly talk, and very little walk. When the preacher would pour out his heart, I often would sit, always on the back seat, listening carefully, and when he finished would ask quietly, "So what? What difference would it make if I were to respond to your invitation?" I watched many others go down front; watched them during the following days and weeks and didn't see any difference in their lives.

When the annual business meeting took place there was little or no evidence that anyone was even a Christian. It was an incredible thing to hear and watch. There weren't too many "happy in the service of the King." From what I saw, the King wasn't very happy with all the proceedings. So I listened, and the bottom line response was, "So what?"

I was recently scheduled to speak on Easter Sunday morning. During the preliminaries leading up to the message, we heard all the Easter, or resurrection songs, and slogans. We read the so-called "Easter" story from the Scripture, and sang the customary songs that relate to the resurrection. "Up from the grave He arose," we sang lustily. My response hadn't changed much in that service, and I found myself asking the question again, "So what?"

When I finally was introduced as the guest speaker, I reminded the audience of all that had been said and sung. Then I just looked at them and asked, "So what? What difference does it make that He died and rose again? What difference does His resurrection make in your life on Monday morning as you roll out of bed and eventually head for work? So what, that He is alive?"

I wish I could describe the looks on the faces of that audience. "How dare you question us like that?" Looks of anger filled with questions of, "Where did they find this guy, and who invited him to preach this morning?" But really, what difference does it make that He is alive? Unless we have discovered the reason the Father raised Him from the dead was to impart His life to us in order to live His life *in* us.

Paul said in Ephesians 2:5, AMP, "Even when we were dead [slain] by [our own] shortcomings and trespasses, He made us alive together in fellowship and in union with Christ. He gave us the very life of Christ Himself, the same new life with which He quickened Him...." There are those words again, our "new life." He gave us the very life of Christ Himself. For what purpose? To be around us, in front of us, or beside us? No, a thousand times, *NO!* He gave us the very life of Christ because we were dead and needed life. Dead men do not need to be healed, they need to be given life! We need *His* life, and that life is an indwelling life. How could that life be effective in us unless that life *were* on the inside? An external Jesus would be as much help to us as He was to the disciples. It wasn't until He took up residence within them that their lives were changed.

People who are disappointed with God reached that point because the God in whom they believed and in whom they had placed their trust had not performed in their lives up to their standard or requests. After a while, when hearing the various evangelical presentations, they came to the conclusion, "So what? What difference does it make?" I understand those feelings and questionings. I've had a few of my own in the past, but it needn't be that way. It was never His intention to make life miserable for you. If your life is miserable as a Christian, it isn't because Jesus hasn't done anything. It is because somewhere along life's way we have failed to discover the life changing relationship of His indwelling, which allows us to be the vehicle through which His life flows unrestricted and unhindered to the ultimate conclusion of fruition. It doesn't mean that we will have a problem-free life. It does mean that in the midst of whatever problem, no matter how great or small, He is big enough to handle it, and at the same time express His joy and peace within you.

It is Jesus who has life, He alone is life. He has come to impart and implant that life *in* us, and He has done just that. There isn't a "So what?" question to that reality. Apart from Him indwelling our humanity, life has no meaning. When He comes to indwell us and we discover that relationship, the question is not "So what?" The question is, "Now what, Lord? What do You want to do with me, in, and through me, now? Furthermore, Lord, it doesn't matter what You do to me, with me, or through me, all that matters is *You.*" You see, the Christian world is so busy trying to live *for* Jesus that they haven't gotten around to discover that He lives *in* them, much less what He would like to do through them.

On a spring Sunday morning, a very distinguished gentleman and what looked to be his son, came into our church. I noticed them immediately as the ministerial team took their places on the platform. He had an incredible head of silver hair, wearing a blue serge suit along with a very smartly dressed ten-year-old son. I watched him as I preached. He in turn was watching me, and every once in a while would turn and look around at other people. The service finished and he introduced himself to me at the door. I had no idea who he was or where he had come from. He continued coming, and three or four weeks later, on the way out of church, he said to me with tears streaming down his cheeks, "I've never heard anything like this in my whole life," and with that immediately left the building.

I said to my wife, "I need to talk to him." I caught up with him in the parking lot, we chatted briefly, and I finally asked him if he had ever invited Jesus Christ into his life. He responded that he had prayed that final prayer with me. We spoke further, and without a shadow of a doubt, he had invited Jesus Christ into his life that Sunday morning.

A few weeks went by. Bill called me and asked that we have lunch that week. We set up a day and met. He started out the conversation by saying, "I have a problem."

I asked, "Really, only one? What's the problem?"

He replied, "I smoke."

I said, "Really, no kidding? What do you want me to do about it?"

He continued, "What should I do about it?"

I responded, "Has anyone in the congregation suggested to you that because you are now a Christian, you should quit smoking as one of the immediate priorities of your life?"

"No," he answered, "But what should I do?"

"What do you think you should do?" I asked.

"I think I should quit."

"Then quit." Simple as that, and he did.

The same exchange took place between us as it related to his drinking problem. No big deal for Bill. It was just a matter of having discovered that the Lord Jesus had come into his life. He wanted more than anything for Christ to control his life, and was perfectly willing to submit to Him on any issue. He discovered the reality of an indwelling Lord Jesus. At that point in time, he knew nothing of what it meant to be crucified with Christ. He knew nothing of the theology behind the relationship. All he knew was that the Lord Jesus had stepped out of eternity into time. He had come to live and indwell him, and promised never to leave him, or forsake him, and he simply said, "Thank You."

As it turned out, the reason they started coming to church in the first place was due to the fact that his son had come home school one afternoon and asked, "Who are Peter and Paul?" Bill didn't have an answer, and wasn't interested. Young Rob pursued the question. Finally, his mother called from the kitchen, "They are part of a singing group called Peter, Paul and Mary."

He said, "No, this Peter and Paul are in the Bible. I just want to know something about them."

Bill responded, "Would you like to go to church so we can find out who Peter and Paul are?"

"Yes, I would," answered Rob, and there they were that first Sunday morning, and the rest is history.

Bill, at that time in his life, was director of sales for the Del Monte Food Corporation. He is retired now, but not before he became one of the vice presidents in charge of sales and now lives in Chesapeake, Virginia.

Don't say "So what?" to Bill. He made the discovery of his life that day when Jesus not only forgave him and changed his eternal destiny from hell to heaven, but He came to live within and he has never been the same. I have watched him down through the years in the midst of good times and adversity, and it has been amazing to watch God at work in his life. Bill and Sallie have known more adversity than the average couple. To begin with, Sallie was born to deaf parents. As a hearing child growing up with deaf parents, it was difficult to say the least. She never in her life went to church where anyone declared the Gospel by voice. In a church full of hearing impaired people, she was assigned to the balcony along with a couple of other non-hearing children to play games, and have a jolly good time.

Some years after they had come to Christ, Sallie became quite ill. Among the problems was lung cancer, a massive heart attack, and later a severe stroke that left her speechless and totally paralyzed on her left side. Her speech eventually came back, and in sharing some of this with us in quite some detail she said in her lovely Virginia drawl, with laughter in her voice, "You know, if God isn't careful, one of these times He's going to kill me!"

In all these years, I have never heard either Bill or Sallie express disappointment with God. I have never heard either of them question, "Where is God? Why is He silent? Why is God hiding from me? Why doesn't He do something?" It never occurred to them; want to know why? They have discovered the liberating life of the indwelling Lord Jesus. They have discovered what it means to have Him as absolute Lord of their lives. When He is operating as absolute Lord in their lives, they needn't question or wonder what He is or isn't doing. It is called the privilege of trusting Him in the midst of adversity. They didn't exercise their so-called authority, for they have none. They simply, deliberately chose to trust Him, knowing that He is more than adequate.

At the moment of this writing, I have talked with them on the telephone and heard the news that Bill, already having lost one kidney, was on the verge of losing the other one. There was no whining or complaining about their situation. Only an attitude of praise and trust, knowing that He is big enough to handle their present circumstances.

One doesn't hear much about that these days. One mostly hears that if you are ill, just remember, God doesn't want anybody sick. If you are ill it is due to one of several things. You probably don't have enough faith or haven't claimed it properly. You might not have confessed in a proper manner, or a hundred and one other things. I've heard all of the above and more.

What a joy to submit to His authority, to His activity, to Him who indwells us. This One, who not only is the Creator, but the Christ of God who gave His life on the cross in order to give us His life. Regardless of what happens to us in life, we needn't be disappointed with God, for we can say with Paul from Romans 8:28, "And we know that all things work together for good...." We know. *We know!* Rather than expressing doubt and depression, "So what?" It is now, "So *now* what, Lord? Whatever it is, it's all right. I look forward in eager expectancy to all that You have in mind to do within, and through me, thank You!"

This is why the apostle Paul wrote in his letter to the Philippians, chapter 1, verse 6, "Being confident of this very thing, that he which hath begun a good work in you will perform it until the day of Jesus Christ." This is why he wrote in 2 Corinthians 12:10, AMP, "So for the sake of Christ, I am well pleased and take pleasure in infirmities, insults, hardships, persecutions, perplexities and distresses; for when I am weak [in human strength], then am I [truly] strong — able, powerful in divine strength." Paul was either some kind of nut or he knew something that most Christians don't know anything about.

Do you know? Do you know what it is when in the midst of adversity to just step back and say, "Lord Jesus, I have no idea what this is all about, but my deliberate choice is, I am going to trust You. Thank You!"

Don't Get Stuck

The Lord Jesus was born, lived, crucified, and the Father raised Him from the grave and He ultimately ascended back to His Father. Shortly thereafter, He descended in the person of His other self, the Holy Spirit, on the day of Pentecost, and took up residence upon and more particularly, within the disciples. In that moment of time, a new relationship was created within the disciples. No longer was He going to be *with* them; but rather, He was living *within* them. That is called a relationship.

In Matthew 1:23, when the angel appeared to Joseph in a dream announcing the birth of the Lord Jesus through Mary, he said, "...They shall call his name Emmanuel, which being interpreted is, God with us." This is the only time in Scripture that the word "Emmanuel" is to be found. It's easily understood why His name would be "Emmanuel," or "God with us." For the first time in the history of man, God is coming down in the form of man to be *with* His people. He was *with* them for a period of 33 years. Toward the end of those years, He gathered His disciples around Him. On several occasions He said to them that He was going to leave them, but would eventually come back and take up residence within them. As I have noted, on the day of Pentecost, He did just that. A new and different relationship, no longer just with them, but *within* His own people. The Lord Jesus is alive and *within* the believer. At that moment in time, the day of Pentecost, the relationship radically changed.

However, unless and until the Lord Jesus, by His Holy Spirit, allows us to see that incredible truth of His indwelling, then that truth remains encased in itself. For you see, I cannot reveal that truth. I can tell you about it, write about it, preach about it, but I cannot reveal it to you; this takes God. Nearly every Christian I have ever talked to says to me, "I know that truth, what's the big deal?"

Shortly after I began to discover the truth of His indwelling, I was so excited I wanted to tell everybody, and in general became a nuisance. I decided to share it with a very close pastoral friend.

At the next pastor's conference, I took my friend aside and said, " You will never guess what I have just discovered."

He asked, "Like what?"

"I have just discovered that the Lord Jesus is alive, and more than that I have discovered that He is right now, living *in* me!"

He gave me a sort of quizzical look and said, "You know, we have been having the nicest weather. It doesn't get any better than this." I was totally devastated to realize that he wasn't the slightest bit interested in this incredible, life changing truth of His indwelling. I dropped the subject.

A few months later we were at another pastor's meeting and again I took him aside, he being one of two very close pastor friends, and once again approached the subject of His indwelling. I was so excited. Again he diverted the conversation to some mundane, didn't matter subject. I was crushed. I could not believe that he would not be interested enough to at least discuss the facts of that relationship. He was not the slightest bit interested.

A few months passed and I received a phone call from a friend who told me that my pastor friend was in the mental ward at the university hospital. I went immediately to his home first, to talk with his wife and learn of the details, with the intention of going on to the hospital to see him. I arrived at his house and knocked on the door. To my utter amazement, my friend answered the door! When he saw it was me he nearly fell to the floor. He broke into great heaves of sobbing tears, and slumped into a chair. I sat next to him, put my arm around him and just began to pray something like, "Lord Jesus, I do not know what the problem is, but I am sure that You do and I am trusting You for the immediate and final outcome of this situation. Amen."

We chatted for two or three hours. The main source of his problem was that he had been eagerly busy for the Lord, and there wasn't any fruit to show for his labor. He shared with me that a few weeks previous, on a Sunday morning, the choir and everyone were about to file into the main sanctuary as the morning worship hour was about to begin. As was his custom, he let everyone go in front of him and he was to be the last one in. Everyone took their place and waited for the pastor to come in. He didn't come.

They waited and waited...no pastor. The organist, which happened to be the pastor's wife, played on. Finally someone went out the door everyone had come in. There he was, in the corner, curled in the fetal position, sobbing uncontrollably.

He said, "Bob, I have been in such depression and stress. I have been so busy for the Lord, but at this point in time, I'm not sure that I'm even a Christian." This was devastating to say the least.

I went to his home on successive Mondays for several weeks, and each time I would share the wonderful truth of Christ's indwelling. How the Lord Jesus not only died for us to take away our sins, changing our destiny and destination from hell to heaven, but that right now He lives *in* you. His response was always the same, "Yes, I know, Bob, you told me that last week."

I continued to share with him of His indwelling, pointing out Colossians 1:27 and Galatians 2:20, among many others. He would always say, "I know those verses, I memorized them several years ago. What do they have to do with me?"

Three or four months passed. One day I received a phone call from a very excited person screaming through the telephone, "Bob, do you know what I just found out?"

I said, "No, but who is this speaking, please?" He identified himself as my good friend, the pastor. I couldn't believe my ears!

He went on to say, excitedly, "I have just found out that Jesus Christ is alive and living *within* me!"

I asked, "How did you find out? Who told you that?"

"I don't know. All I know is that I now know that He is living within me!" he replied.

I had been telling him for weeks, and he thought he knew. Now the Holy Spirit opened his eyes and allowed him to see for the first time in his life that the Lord Jesus was indeed living *in* him. Who told him that? Well, I had, but it took the Holy Spirit to "reveal," or as I said in an earlier chapter, to "take the cover off."

There is no way that I can diagram this relationship for you. I cannot set up a seminar and give you the 1, 2, 3's, or A, B, C's of this relationship. You cannot diagram it, or define it in an analytical sense of the word. It takes the Holy Spirit to open the heart and allow someone to *see* the truth.

Oftentimes, He allows those to see who have been going through insurmountable stress, turmoil, and suffering. It is said of the Lord Jesus, in Hebrews 5:8 from the Amplified translation, "Although He was a Son, He learned [active, special] obedience through what He suffered." One of the reasons for suffering is to finally bring us to the absolute end of ourselves, where we are prepared to put away all self-defense and argument, and just be open to the Spirit's ministry. We can know the truth academically, intellectually, theologically, and perfectly. But there is a difference between knowing the truth in that manner, and *knowing* the truth.

One of the great problems in anyone discovering the liberating truth of His indwelling, is that we tend to get stuck in certain areas of truth. For example, every Christian knows, and will agree that the Lord Jesus was born in Bethlehem. Praise God for His miraculous birth, that He was willing to be born as one of us! We can never thank Him enough. But it is tragic if one finds himself stuck at that point in his life. Yet for many who call themselves

Christians, the most important part of Jesus is His birth. Consequently, when Christmas arrives, people get all excited about the baby Jesus.

Then there are others who would say, "No, His birth isn't enough, He didn't stop there. He lived a sinless life, and as such is our model to live by. He's our example of living and we must strive to follow His example." Years ago, one of the favorite hymns in our church was "Trying to Walk in the Steps of the Saviour." As a child walking through the snow following your father, have you ever tried to walk in his steps? It isn't difficult, it's impossible. Yet the portrayal of the Christian life for many, is this procedure of trying to follow His example and walk in His steps. They are stuck at that point in time of the life of Jesus.

Others would say, "Oh no, we don't stop with His life, He was crucified. He gave His life for our sins." Many at that point would go on to say, "And that's not all, He was buried and rose again the third day. He was resurrected from the dead." They would be right and we are profoundly grateful for His death, burial, and resurrection. However, many get "stuck" at the point of His crucifixion. Intellectually, they agree that He was buried and raised again from the grave, but for all practical purposes He was crucified, and that's all. Christianity is taken up with the crucifixion. Genuine, born-again Christians wear the cross on a chain around their necks. Others will wear a cross with Jesus still hanging on it on a chain around their neck. Stuck at the cross. The songwriter wrote for many, their favorite hymn, "Old Rugged Cross." Part of the chorus says, "And I'll cling to the old rugged cross, and exchange it some day for a crown." Have you ever read anything in Scripture about doing that?

It is one thing to be on the right side of the crucifixion, but on the wrong side of the resurrection. One can be on the right side of the resurrection, but on the wrong side of the ascension; or be on the right side of the ascension, but on the wrong side of His descent on the day of Pentecost. It took it *all* in order for Him to establish that relationship of which He spoke in John's gospel to the disciples, "I am going to be *in* you and you *in* Me" (John 14:20).

It's absolutely imperative that we do not get "stuck" at one particular point in the life of Christ, but rather that our focus be upon *Him*, and Him alone. It is difficult to discover true focus in the first place, and tough to remain focused upon Him. For example, we discover the "indwelling" of the Lord Jesus and begin to worship the "indwelling." It's easy to get "stuck" on His indwelling and forget all about Him. Is His indwelling important? Absolutely! But don't get stuck there. *He* is what is important. People discover their "oneness in Christ," get stuck on their "oneness," and forget all about Him.

He is what is important. The most wonderful, thrilling discovery one can make that He is living *within* us, and ready and waiting to live out His life through us.

14

Wow!

I would imagine that most everyone who will read this book is familiar with the story of the woman at the well. If you don't know, you will find it recorded in John's gospel, chapter 4. The story is of an encounter Jesus had with a Samaritan woman. When Jesus asked her for a drink, it really surprised her, for in her own words she said, "...How is it that thou being a Jew, askest drink of me, which am a woman of Samaria? for the Jews have no dealings with the Samaritans" (verse 9).

In the process of that exchange Jesus said to her, "...The water that I shall give him shall be in him a well of water springing up into everlasting life" (John 4:14b). *Wow!* The most totally unimaginable, unthinkable, unbelievable thing that could ever be spoken, has now just been spoken to a woman who had been married five times, and was now living with the sixth man! A woman totally destitute of anything called value, honesty, integrity, truth, and love, is being told that He would not only give her a drink, but a drink of a kind of water the likes of which she could never imagine. A drink that would change her life as well as her life-style. Furthermore, that drink of water would be *in* her a well of water springing up into life everlasting. That kind of life would not be just durational life, but *His* life...the very life of God.

Having been a pastor for many years, it was my responsibility and joy to perform many weddings. After a great deal of counseling, I would seek from the couple their thoughts about sharing with the audience just preceding the actual marriage vows, a short message of what it means to know Jesus Christ. Without exception every couple responded positively, and as a matter of fact eagerly, because of the possibility of someone being there that didn't know Him.

On one particular occasion, I shared briefly what it meant to invite the Lord Jesus into one's life. When the wedding was finished, the people were gathered in the fellowship hall. I finished my duties and joined them. In the process of milling about, a little boy approached me and asked, "Are you the preacher here?"

I answered, "Yes, as a matter of fact, I am."

"I really did like your sermon," he said. When does a preacher hear that from a nine year old!

Being a bit flattered, I asked, "What did you like about it?"

His response was very quick, "It was short."

Having the bubble of my ego burst by a little boy, I finally mustered up enough courage to ask another question, "Was there anything else that you liked about it?"

He answered, "As a matter of fact there was. I liked that part about inviting Jesus into my life."

I was stunned by his response, but continued by asking, "Have you ever invited Jesus into your life?"

"Sure, lots of times," was his reply.

Of course, that was the wrong answer to that question, so I pursued the conversation by sharing with him that once you have invited Jesus Christ to come and live in you, He will come at your invitation. I asked him, "Would you like to invite Him into your life, right now?"

To my amazement, he answered, "Yes, I would." I shared briefly with him a little prayer that I would pray, and that he could pray after me. Very simply and gently, I prayed the prayer to receive the Lord Jesus. He very carefully prayed each word.

By this time, I knew that his name was Anthony, and I said, "Anthony, did you invite Jesus to come and live in you?"

He replied, "Yes, I did."

"Did He come in?"

With a puzzled look on his face he said, "I think so, I hope so." I explained that the moment he had invited the Lord Jesus to come in, His promise is that He would come in. John 1:12 makes that quite clear, and I showed him that passage. "Anthony, the Bible also says that once He comes to live in you, His promise is that He will never leave you, nor forsake you" (Hebrews 13:5).

All the while we were talking, people were milling about. We were standing in the center of all the activity, and I said to him, "He has promised that He has come in and He will never, never, never leave you, or forsake you."

He paused for a moment, and with eyes glistening looked into my eyes and said, "Wow!"

"Wow" is right!

Do you remember when you invited the Lord Jesus into your life? If you can't remember that, then you haven't invited Him in. It is rather a simple principle. When a person invites the Lord Jesus to come in, it is something to be remembered. I often ask people who are married if they remember being married. "Do you remember the day when you were married?"

"Well, of course, I remember that day, how could I forget?" That is precisely the point. If you have ever invited Him into your life, there should be no doubt about it. You were there when it happened and you ought to know. If there is any doubt in your mind, reader friend of mine, you can stop for a moment right now, and as Anthony did, just receive Him into your life. As I reassured Anthony, I can reassure you that the moment you invite Him to come into your life, at that moment He steps out of eternity into time, into your life *never* to leave you nor forsake you, *never*!

Someone said to me once upon hearing that, "Yes, but I can leave Him."

I said, "Really, where would you go?" The Psalmist declares, in Psalm 139:7, "Whither shall I go from thy spirit? or whither shall I flee from thy presence?"

It's impossible to leave God or to get out of His presence. You can ignore Him, get out of fellowship with Him, but once He comes in He doesn't begin a process of jumping in and out of your life each and every time you happen to sin. If that were the case, He would be most busy jumping in and out, for you sin a lot more than you would be prepared to admit. Even when we think we are not sinning we probably are, because of our pride in thinking we are not!

But, WOW! Remember when you invited Him into your life? I realize there are different responses to His incoming. For the most part, people are thrilled to bits when they discover that their sins are forgiven, and are now bound for heaven having had their names written down in the Lamb's book of life! WOW! Unfortunately, that "wow" seems to last for only a little while. We all know that. It dissipates, and finally disappears into the sunset. Mind you, we're still Christians. We have learned the language. We can pray with the best of them because we have listened to others pray and have picked up the necessary language and phrases. The "wow" is now "woe," and sometimes, "gloom, despair, and agony...oh me!"

Of course, we can do as Moses did in Exodus 34:33. "He put a veil on his face." Paul tells us the reason he did that in 2 Corinthians 3:13, AMP, "...Who put a veil over his face so that the Israelites might not gaze upon the finish of the vanishing [splendor which had been upon it]." Simply, he did not want the Israelites to know that the glow had vanished. The "wow" was no more.

In a Bible Conference in northern Wisconsin a few years ago, I was preaching about this subject of the Lord Jesus living within us, and the joy of that relationship. In the process of that conference a man came to me and said, "I know what you are talking about, but something has happened, I don't have it anymore. I remember the first days after inviting Jesus to come in. They were so wonderful and exciting, but now it is all problems and confusion, difficulties and stress," and on and on he went.

By his own admission, he had not been involved in any great sin or sins. He loved God and his family. He loved his church, but there was no joy and happiness. He asked, "Why?"

I took him back to when he invited Jesus into his life, and sure enough it had been a genuine invitation. "I think what has happened is that you have gotten really busy *for* Jesus, and through the process of time haven't discovered how to let Jesus be busy *through* you. They are not the same, you know." It was with great joy to share with him what it means to have Him living within us, and through us, and all we need to do is let Him!

When we finally finished our conversation, all he could say, with his Hispanic accent, was, "Press [praise] the Lord! Press the Lord! Press His Holy Name! He lives within me! He lives within me!" Talk about excited, this man was excited. *Wow!*

I have had the privilege of travelling throughout the United States, Canada, and around the world preaching in every conceivable kind of Bible conference and church. Rarely do you find anyone who is excited about the Lord Jesus. It is extremely rare to find someone who is excited about the indwelling reality of the Lord Jesus and about what He is doing in their lives. If they are excited, it is usually because of what they are trying to do *for* the Lord.

A few years ago I received two 60-minute tapes from a missionary friend of mine in Papua, New Guinea. The missionaries were having their annual conference in Goroka, New Guinea, to give reports on all the work going on in their various stations.

One young missionary stood and shared that he and his wife, and another couple, had been with a tribe called the Bisorio Indians in a very remote part of that country. They had no idea where and how to start their ministry. It was obvious that it would take time to learn the language and after several years they felt ready.

They approached the chief and asked him if they could have an hour a week of "big talk" with the people. I'm sure you know what "big talk" would be. Have you ever engaged in "small talk"? "Small talk" is that conversation that doesn't amount to anything important. "Big talk" would be that talk of great concern and importance. The chief, without hesitation said, "No." When asked why, he responded, "If you had wanted to have big talk with us you wouldn't have asked for just an hour a week. Your big talk is not big talk at all, it is small talk." So he refused.

The missionaries came back in a day or two and asked for permission for "big talk" not for just an hour a week, but rather for an hour every day. The chief responded happily, "Yes, that would be good. When do you want to start?"

"We will let you know."

The missionary continued, "The reason we said we would let him know was because we didn't know how we were going to approach this extraordinary opportunity." The missionaries, two couples, talked among themselves as to what and how they would present the Gospel. It was an unbelievable struggle to discern what would be the best approach.

After much prayer and discussion, one of them finally came up with what he thought was a great idea, "Why don't we begin where God began, with creation?" What a novel idea...so simple. They all agreed it was a great plan.

Next problem, "What method are we going to use to present the Gospel? A discussion group?" That wouldn't work, no one there knew anything about the Bible.

"Should we use a lecture format?" one of them asked. That was too formal, they decided. Finally, they hit on the idea of presenting the Gospel by means of drama. They would drama-tize their presentation. Again, after much discussion and prayer, it was decided to use that method for their presentation.

They notified the chief that they would begin in a few days, and shortly thereafter they began with the book of Genesis. Their first lesson was as in the Bible: Creation. God created the world, man, and woman. They sensed an incredible presence of the Spirit. When they finished, the tribe was so responsive, saying to them, "We must belong to God."

"Why?" the missionaries asked.

"Because whenever one of us makes something, a tool or what-ever, the one that makes it, he is the creator and owner of that object. If God created us, made us, then we must belong to God."

94

Assuring them that this, in a broad sense is true, they went to their huts and homes to praise Him for the start, and for the way that He would continue in the days and months ahead. Personally, I cannot imagine undertaking such a project. The hours and hours that it would take daily to get ready for the next day, but they did it.

There were many mood swings as one can imagine. For example, when they dealt with Adam's sin and fall. How does one dramatize the fall of man...the total sinfulness of man? Amazing! But they, faithful to the Word and each day, dramatized the Scriptures to the tribe.

They finally reached the New Testament and the birth of Jesus was dramatized. The tribe was ecstatic! "It is difficult to describe," the missionaries reported. They continued through the New Testament, and eventually came to the crucifixion. When "big talk" finished on that day the tribe was filled with gloom and despair. The tribe declared, "Jesus, the Son of God, is dead." They were filled with sadness.

The missionaries announced, "We will not have 'big talk' for two days." The tribe murmured among themselves for the next two days. The missionaries were nowhere to be seen.

Finally, the announcement, "Big talk, tomorrow morning, the third morning, at dawn."

Long before dawn, the tribe assembled for "big talk." The resurrection of Jesus was portrayed through drama before the tribe. As they sat breathless, the announcement was given, "Jesus, the Son of God, has been raised from the dead. He is no longer in the grave and is now alive!"

A loud, thunderous cheer went up from the tribe, "Jesus is alive! Jesus is alive!" For the whole day the people shouted and rejoiced over the fact that Jesus is alive.

In the days that followed, the missionaries drove home the reason for the Son of God being crucified and raised from the dead. They focused on the truth of His ascension, and ultimate descent of the Holy Spirit to take up residence in their lives for the purpose of living His life through them. In time, they were given the privilege of inviting the Lord Jesus into their lives.

Their report concluded by saying all but one old man responded and invited the Lord Jesus into their lives! The old man was seen gathering up his meager belongings and leaving the tribe.

As tremendous and unimaginable as this account is, their closing statement of the tape was the most insightful and revealing. It was, "All the time during the months of preparation and dramatizing the Gospel, we felt as though we were on the sidelines just watching what the Lord was doing."

That's the Gospel! That is what the Gospel is about! The Gospel isn't what they, as missionaries, can do *for* Jesus. It is what He can do within and through them. The Gospel isn't what you can do *for* Him. It is what He can do in you and through you. "*Wow!*"

Do you know anything about this "*wow*," or has your so-called Christian life turned into "*woe*"? It is absolutely amazing how many Christians are living a *woe*-full life, going through the motions, using all the Christian vocabulary, but deep inside there is near nothing. Some have the faintest memory of their conversion experience and thrill that was present upon inviting Him into their lives. It is a sad thing to walk into some churches and find such an evident lack of joy and life.

I heard a story not long ago of a man who had a heart attack in church, and it was said that the paramedics came and carried out the last three rows before they found the dead man! It seemed humorous at first, but in fact there was too much truth to it. For you see, Jesus could die and most churches wouldn't miss Him! The service would continue and conclude just as it has in the past. What a pity.

Jesus said, "I am come that they might have life, and that they might have it more abundantly" (John 10:10). Remember the woman at the well, "Whosoever drinketh of the water that I shall give him shall never thirst; but the water that I shall give him shall be *in* him a well of water springing up into everlasting life" (John 4:14).

These are not just words or promises to be underlined in yellow, these are *His* words, *His* promises, and He lives *in* you and me to produce within and through us what *He* promised. *"Wow!"*

Why isn't there more evidence of His life and joy in the fellowship of believers? It is for the same reason that the Lord Jesus said to the church at Ephesus in Revelation 2:2, "I know thy works, and thy labour, and thy patience, and how thou canst not bear them which are evil."

In 1 Thessalonians 1:3, Paul remembered, "...Your work of faith, and labour of love, and patience of hope in our Lord Jesus Christ...." In the church at Ephesus there was no faith to explain it; no love to compel it; no hope to sustain it. Consequently, the Lord said to the Ephesian church, verse 4, "I have this against you, because you have left your first love. Therefore, repent."

Without a doubt, they had their doctrine straight. They knew whom to expel from their fellowship in order to keep the fellowship pure. They knew what to believe and what not to believe in a dogmatic manner, but had left their first love!

Plenty of works, but no faith!

Plenty of labor, but no love!

Plenty of patience, but no hope!

He said, *repent!* Get back to Jesus, and Jesus alone. It was Vance Havner, that great southern preacher who said, "If you get past Jesus, you're too far past!" The church of Jesus Christ has gotten past Jesus. We just use Him to try and get what we want, when we want it, and how we want it. If He is not forthcoming with our requests and sometimes demands, we get discouraged and disappointed with Jesus. Poor little me!

The Lord Jesus gave His life on the cross in order to give us His life. Because we were dead in trespasses and sins (Ephesians 2:1) and needed life, He gave His life to us. He now indwells us with His life ready to live that life out through us. What can we say but "thank You"? "Thank You, Lord Jesus, for coming to live *in* me! Thank You, Lord Jesus, for living through me. I don't know how You are going to do it, but thank *You*."

If you pray a prayer like that, be careful, He is listening. *"Wow!"*

15

The Risk Factor

The question that always comes after a presentation of the truth of His indwelling is, "What is the risk involved in giving Him my life?"

My question to them is, "What is the risk in *not* giving Him my life?" Keep in mind that we are not really giving Him anything, much less our lives. The Lord Jesus, by virtue of His birth, life, death, burial, and resurrection *bought* us. We are His purchased possession.

Paul addressed this issue when he wrote to the Corinthians in his second epistle, the last two verses of chapter six, "What? know ye not that your body is the temple of the Holy Ghost which is in you, which ye have of God, and ye are not your own? For ye are bought with a price" (1 Corinthians 6:19-20a).

We Christians have confused the issue, regardless of whose fault it is. The fact is, that the Lord Jesus *bought* us with His blood. We are His purchased possession. We belong to Him. As His purchased possession, as His property, we have no option but to obey Him. We have so twisted this truth that we have come to believe the opposite. "We are who we are, because of what we are." Now that we have become Christians it is up to us to somehow please God with what we do and say. Consequently, the harder we try the more we fail.

We often hear people pray, "Lord, we thank You for the privilege of coming to *Your* house today," referring to the church building. The reality is that the church building, or main sanctuary, is not the *house* of God. Our bodies are the *main* sanctuary. Our bodies are the *house* of God. Yet, no one says anything...we just listen and take it hook, line, and sinker.

Does it make any difference? It is the difference between day and night. The difference between discovering the reality of an indwelling Lord Jesus within *this house*, or just continue to do the best we can until Jesus comes, and miss the total purpose for which He died.

In our attempt to exhibit the Lord Jesus in our lives, we have failed to discover that it is an exercise in utter futility. We need to examine the language of the relationship that we have in Christ before we can ever expect to exhibit the life of the Lord Jesus in that relationship.

Psalm 23, that great shepherd psalm, has been relegated to the funeral. However, it is not a death psalm. It is a life psalm.

The phrase in verse six brings life into focus for the rest of the Psalm when David says, "Surely goodness and mercy shall follow me *all the days of my life....*" Link that phrase with every other phrase of that Psalm and you will see it open before your eyes like the beauty and fragrance of a blooming rose.

He is my Shepherd...all the days of my life. As my Shepherd, He has made every provision for me, as one of His sheep, for every conceivable problem that would ever develop in my life...all the days of my life. What is so incredible is that the Shepherd is not an external shepherd. This Shepherd, the Lord Jesus Christ, has taken up residence *within*. The fullness and overwhelming completeness of the Shepherd has come to dwell *in* me...all the days of my life.

No wonder David could conclude, "I shall not want." Have you ever heard anyone pray, "Lord Jesus, I am so excited about the fact that You are alive and living in me. You have provided everything that I will need today for every situation with which I will be confronted. Today you have already made provision for those situations, and I just want to tell You, *I have no wants today!* You can do with me what You jolly well please. Take me anywhere You want to take me, whatever, wherever, bump into whomever. You do with, in, and through me, whatever You would like to do, and I will live today in utter expectation and anticipation for what that might be. Thanks in advance for what You are going to do!" Ever heard anybody pray like that? Probably not. Why? Because we do not really know the *indwelling* Shepherd.

Examine the language of your prayer life. Is it a constant barrage to God of all your hurts and ills, your gripes and wants, your grocery list? People often come to me and ask me to pray for them. I usually ask, "What is it, exactly, that you want me to tell God to do on your behalf?" For you see, that is usually what prayer is about.

Examine your "Christian" language. Is it about an external Jesus whom you are serving? Search your "Christian" hymns and choruses. Are they songs that constantly refer to an external Jesus? Is He a Jesus that you are trying to follow around...or neatly beside you? Is He there only to comfort and encourage you...to do your bidding? Jesus didn't die on a cross for that purpose. He died to become your indwelling, total Provider and Shepherd, and we live as though He didn't exist.

I remember discovering the 23rd Psalm and some of these truths for the first time, nearly 40 years ago and crying out to the Lord, "Lord Jesus, I want to know something of Your shepherdship. I want to know the reality of Your indwelling." And the wee, still, small voice of the Spirit said, "Read on."

Psalm 23, verse 2, "He maketh me to lie down in green pastures." I thought, "What in the world is that about?" That is about submission. The position of lying down is the position of submission. I hate submission. Submitting to my mother, brother and sisters was not on my agenda. The last thing I would have ever wanted to do was to submit to them or anyone else for that matter. Consequently, when it came to submitting to the Lord, I had great difficulty.

Look at the verse, "Lie down in green pastures." It is not His purpose to rip and tear out of our lives those lovely things that He has provided. On the contrary, He wants to take those things, enhance them, increase them for our own enjoyment and encouragement. Submission to Him is not a chore, it is a choice. The choice of experiencing Christ at work within and through us. Let the green pastures roll...let them come, I am ready and expectant!

"He leadeth me beside still waters," I read. What does that mean? Once again it speaks of submission. "Oh, brother, not that again. Can't we just submit one time and have it over with?" I thought. Then I remembered, "All the days of my life." "Still waters?" Not stagnant waters...still waters. Ah, you see, the body of water that runs deep and wide is the body of water that possesses incredible unlimited power and strength.

You see what He is saying? The Shepherd, the indwelling Shepherd, is saying that if you are prepared to discover what submission really is, He is prepared to introduce you to a life of such great reality, power, and blessing that it is beyond your wildest imagination!

That's not all! "He restoreth my soul." That is that part of you made up of your mind, emotions, and will. God made us body, soul, and spirit. He told Adam and Eve, after showing them around the Garden of Eden, "You can eat of any and all of the fruit that is before you, but of the tree of knowledge of good and evil, you shall not eat of it. If you do, you will surely die."

Eat they did, and die they did. Oh, not immediately or physically. The death of which He spoke was a spiritual death. That is, He withdrew Himself, His Holy Spirit from their human spirit and left them dead spiritually. His Holy Spirit indwelt their human spirit for the purpose of giving them the joy of submitting to Him in all they did or said. With their minds they could communicate with each other and with Him. They could confide in each other and in Him. Then individually and together they could exercise their will and decide what to do about any decision that needed to be made. They had the choice of whether or not to yield to Him in every situation.

Because of the disobedience in eating of the tree of knowledge of good and evil, the Holy Spirit was withdrawn, and they were left to their own soulish desires of the mind, emotions, and will, without the indwelling Holy Spirit's control.

When the Lord Jesus voluntarily gave His life on the cross for our sins, He made it possible for us to once again receive Him into our lives. When a person receives the Lord Jesus into their life, He comes in the person of His Holy Spirit. He, the Holy Spirit, has been restored to that repentant person and indwells the individual. Restored to function once again as God intended man to function. How was that? We have the Lord Jesus, the Holy Spirit within our human spirit for the purpose of relying upon Him, confiding in Him, trusting Him with each and every situation of life...all the days of our lives!

We have a mind to think about things, to think things through. Our emotions come into obvious play, but ultimately our will decides upon a course of action. He has given us Himself so that we can rely totally upon Him in every situation. Paul called it, "Being filled with the Holy Spirit." He will control only those believers who are "submitted" to Him. Only those believers who "yield" to Him. It started way back in Psalm 23, further back than that, really. But here is the relationship described for us. For David, it was an external relationship. For us today, it is an internal relationship. He has come to reside within.

Examine your "believer" language. Are you still referring to Him as being on the outside? Or is it a conglomeration of inside and outside, as though He is jumping in and out each time you talk or sing of Him. If you never come to a solid conclusion and discover that the Lord Jesus is *within* you, you will never discover the thrilling release of His life through you, not even for a day, much less "all the days of your life."

When I began to discover the truth of this psalm, once I cried to Him, "Lord, I want to know," again, that wee, small voice of the Spirit said, "Read on."

"Yea, though I walk through the valley of the shadow of death, I will fear no evil." Stumped again! What is this about? Usually, this is read at a funeral with a very soft voice with various inflections to make it effective. I know all about that. Yet, what is the meaning and how does it work? Sounds like death is involved. Indeed, it is! Yours and mine! Jesus said in John 12:24, "...Except a corn of wheat fall into the ground and die, it abideth alone: but if it die, it bringeth forth much fruit."

He was referring to His ultimate death. He was also making reference to our identification with Him in that same death. For He knew full well that the only person who could live the Christ life was Himself. He knew that although He would soon take up residence in the lives of believers, they of themselves, were absolutely helpless when it would come to the living out of the Christ life. He knew full well, that in order for Him to live out His life through a human being, it would take the death of that person in order that He might live His life out through the believer.

Paul refers to that in Galatians 2:20 when he said, "I am crucified with Christ: nevertheless I live; yet not I, but Christ liveth in me." We nonchalantly quote that verse without going to the trouble of finding out what it means.

The risk factor? Yes, there is risk. But the risk in not joining Him on the cross to be crucified with Him is far more devastating than not. To join Him on the cross and die is not a risk at all. For it is the Christ, the living, Sovereign, Shepherd, Savior who is living within! Without our death with Him, He cannot and will not live His life in us, much less through us. Death is the dynamic which allows the Lord Jesus to move into action in our lives. This is a personal, private relationship that requires a personal, private act of the will deliberately giving Him the right to exercise His will in and over my life.

When Elijah was about to be taken by a whirlwind, he said to Elisha (2 Kings 2), that the Lord was sending him to Bethel and that he, Elisha, should stay put. Elisha said, "Not a chance, I'm going with you." Do you remember what happened at Bethel? This is God's place of communication! You will find it in Genesis 28. The account of Jacob having a dream. In the dream the Lord said to him (verse 13), "...I am the Lord God of Abraham thy father, and the God of Isaac: the land whereon thou liest, to thee will I give it, and to thy seed." In verse 15, "And, behold, I am with thee, and will keep thee in all places whither thou goest, and will bring thee again into this land; for I will not leave thee, until I have done that which I have spoken to thee of." Naturally, Jacob argued and doubted what the Lord had said to him.

Think about it! At Bethel, this is an exchange between God and a man. This is what God can and did say. And Jacob doubted and argued! He would have made a great present-day Christian.

Elijah said to Elisha (2 Kings 2:4), "The Lord is sending me to Jericho. You stay here."

Elisha said, "Not a chance." So the two of them went on to Jericho. Do you remember what happened at Jericho? That was the place of God's conquest!

The nation of Israel had just come across the Jordan River and was in the process of going on into Canaan. The Lord met with Joshua. "It came to pass, when Joshua was by Jericho, that he lifted up his eyes and looked, and, behold, there stood a man over against him with his sword drawn in his hand: and Joshua went unto him, and said unto him, Art thou for us, or for our adversaries?" (Joshua 5:13).

I first heard this passage preached by Major Ian Thomas seven times in one day. I had the privilege of taking him around to various places in St. Paul, Minnesota. After the day was finished he said to me, "After today, you should know something about Joshua." I have never forgotten what he said.

Joshua asked, "Are you for us or for our adversaries?"

The Lord answered, "No, but as Captain of the host of the Lord, am I now come."

Major Thomas' comment was, "The Lord said, 'I haven't come to take sides. I have come to take over.'" As in Bethel, the place of communication. The place where God demonstrated what He could say. Now at Jericho, the place of conquest. The place where God demonstrated what He could do. Elijah said to Elisha, "The Lord hath sent me to Jordan. You stay here."

Elisha said, "Not a chance." The two of them went on to Jordan. Remember what went on at the Jordan?

That is where Israel left all, everything behind and at God's direction went on in to the land that had been promised them many years before. This was the place of commitment or identification. The place where one says, "I can't do it. I can't do it even with Your help. *You*, God, must do it."

Elijah was taken by a whirlwind into heaven, leaving Elisha standing there in front of all the sons of the prophets...men of the seminary, if you please. The people who knew how to do everything right. The spectators of this world, ready to criticize anyone and everything. Now they are watching what Elisha would do. A tremendous principle here. God is saying through Elijah, I can introduce you to that place of communication. I can remind you of what God can and did say. I can introduce you to that place of conquest. I can remind you of what God can do. I can introduce you and remind you of that place of commitment...that which *you* must do. However, from this point on, you go alone. With that, Elijah was gone. Elisha, left alone before God and the sons of the prophets.

The sons of the prophets, ah, they were that bunch that knew how to do everything. They were especially good at finding fault and criticizing anyone and everything that anyone else brought up. And now, there is Elisha, alone, forsaken by his mentor and from all appearances forsaken by God. He could have panicked. He could have run to the seminarians and begged them to take him in. He cried, "Where is the Lord God of Elijah?" Not, "Where is Elijah?" It didn't matter where Elijah was. What did matter was, "Where is God?" With that, he took the mantle of Elijah and struck the waters of the Jordan. The waters parted, he went over and through the Jordan on dry ground. Elijah could take him just so far. He had to go through the Jordan alone.

This was his personal identification with the God of Elijah. I can take you just so far. I can tell you all about the Christian life, but in the final analysis, you are the one that will have to decide whether or not you want what God wants. Whether or not you are prepared to put everything at His disposal, including your life and everything that pertains to your life and say, "God, my life is Yours. You bought it with the blood of Your Son, the Lord Jesus, and You can do with it and me what You jolly well please." Perhaps for the first time in your life you can begin to enter into the reality of His indwelling. This is what it means to die to self and discover that in dying we begin to live!

The "Rest" Factor . . .
These Are His!

I remember the first time I heard this song,

> *"Jesus, I am resting, resting!*
> *In the joy of what Thou art!*
> *I am finding out the greatness,*
> *Of Thy loving heart."*

As the congregation of nearly 5,000 sang, I looked around at the people and it sounded majestic, triumphant, even restful. As I thought of my own life, I sang a different message,

> "Jesus, I am wrestling, wrestling.
> In the pain of what I am.
> I am finding out how useless,
> How futile, restless, and on and on...."

Of course, my song didn't rhyme. There was no melody or harmony in my life, it didn't need to rhyme. It didn't matter. I had been a pastor for five years telling people how wonderful it was to be saved, to know Jesus, and it didn't matter.

Then I met the Lord Jesus! I discovered His indwelling presence! I realized that He didn't come into my life in order for me to prove that I could perform, in terms of human adequacy. I had already proved that I could not perform...that I was not adequate. For years I had lived with an inferiority complex. Now I was face to face with the reality that it wasn't a complex. I was genuinely inferior. That is why He came into my life, to prove that He was adequate. All I needed to do was to discover how to *rest* in His adequacy.

This is not a sit-down do-nothing rest as some might think. There are those that think that. However, if we are trusting Him to live His life out through us, and others think that nothing is going to happen, that simply means that Jesus is a do-nothing Christ. It couldn't be further from the truth. To rest in Him is to turn Him loose to do whatever He chooses.

Resting in Christ is a conscious act of my will to admit that the totality of my life...all of my rag dolls and plastic horses are *not* mine, but *His*. I do not claim ownership of anything that goes by my name. All that I am, or have ever been, or ever hope to be are *His*. That was determined the day He went to the cross and died for me. It was discovered in my life by a conscious act of my will, to be true. I admitted it before God and anyone else who might have been interested. My life was His life. His life *is* my life. These are not mine...they are *His*!

The apostle Paul declared in Philippians 4:12, AMP, "...I have learned in any and all circumstances, the secret of facing every situation...." What did he know? Obviously, he knew what it was to be a believer. We read about that in Acts, chapter 9, in his encounter with the Lord Jesus. That was the day when he came to know the Lord Jesus as his personal Savior.

I had known Jesus for a number of years and had no idea about knowing any secret of how to face every situation. I didn't know there was a secret. How did I face every situation? Well, it depended upon the circumstances. If it was a mild situation or simple encounter of a problem I could probably "wing it," and get through without too much difficulty. If it was a very difficult situation, and I mean *very*...then it called for "panic." Call out the prayer chain!!! Do whatever was necessary to let people know that I am in deep trouble. Pray for me! Pray for me! *Rest?* Not a chance. *Rest* in Jesus? I didn't know how. What did Paul know that I didn't know? He knew the Lord Jesus as his personal Savior.

What else did he know? He talks about it in Galatians 1:11-12, AMP, "For I want you to know, brethren, that the Gospel which was proclaimed and made known by me is not man's gospel — a human invention, according to or patterned after any human standard. For indeed I did not receive it from man, nor was I taught it; [it came to me] through a [direct] revelation [given] by Jesus Christ, the Messiah."

What do you suppose the revelation was about? He tells us in verse 16, when He, Jesus, "Saw fit and was pleased to reveal [unveil, disclose] His Son WITHIN [capitalization mine] me so that I might proclaim Him among the Gentiles...."

It was the same verbal message Jesus gave to His disciples just before He was crucified. "I am going to come and live *in* you the life that you cannot live." He revealed it to them. Flesh and blood cannot reveal this truth to another. It takes the dynamic of the Holy Spirit to reveal.

Was this all Paul knew in order to say, "I have learned the secret of how to face every situation"? Many people will agree to the fact that Jesus lives in them. I knew that fact during all the stress years. The fact that He lived *in* me meant nothing to me as it related to the problems of my life. So He must have known something more. Indeed He did.

Paul's letter to the Philippians, chapter 2, verse 5, "Let this same attitude and purpose and [humble] mind be in you which was in Christ Jesus." What was this humble mind? It was a disposition which He adopted toward His Father. In an earlier chapter, I said, "That as the Father lived *in* Him, *He* lived *in* His Father." In that relationship, He had the choice as to whether or not He would be prepared to yield to His Father; whether or not He was prepared to be totally dependent upon His Father.

He said in John 5:30, "I can of mine own self do nothing... because I seek not mine own will, but the will of the Father which hath sent me." That was the disposition of which Paul spoke in Philippians 2. He admonishes us to adopt that same disposition.

Paul further describes that disposition that Jesus adopted. Philippians 2:6-8, AMP, "Who, [Jesus], although being essentially one with God and in the form of God [possessing the fullness of the attributes which make God God], did not think this equality with God was a thing to be eagerly grasped or retained." (These are not *mine*...they are *His*.) "But stripped Himself [of all privileges and rightful dignity] so as to assume the guise of a servant (slave), in that He became like men and was born a human being. "And after He had appeared in human form *He* abased and humbled Himself [still further] and carried His obedience to the extreme of death, even the death of [the] cross!" There you have it!

He was fully prepared to live His life in absolute and total abandonment to His Father. Whatever the Father wanted, He wanted. Wherever the Father sent Him, He went. No questions asked, total obedience! Total abandonment!

I met a young man who was a champion downhill skier for Canada. He attended some meetings where I was preaching and approached me one evening after the service. We chatted a bit and finally agreed to meet the next day for lunch and discuss further the subject of "Christ living in us."

We met the next day and I asked the first question, "What is it like to be on the top of a mountain, in the starting gate, listening to the countdown for the beginning of your attempt at skiing down that massive mountain?"

He answered, "As I wait, 10...9...8...I mentally wind up every muscle in my body in anticipation of the 3...2...1..., and then I totally abandon myself to the hill."

In the process of our discussion, I said, "This whole principle of allowing Jesus Christ to live His life out through you requires the same disposition to Him, as your disposition was in the race and to the mountain, total abandonment to Him." No reservation, total abandonment!

The Holy Spirit writing through Paul says to us, "As He adopted that disposition of total dependence and abandonment to His Father, we now have the privilege of abandoning ourselves to the Lord Jesus." However, as long as we are in the "these are mine" mood and syndrome, we will never ever entertain the slightest hint or desire to do so.

What was Paul's response to his own admonition? Read about it in Philippians 3:7, AMP, "But whatever former things I had that might have been gains to me...." What former things?

Verse 5, *his pride of ancestry*, "Circumcised when I was eight days old, of the race of Israel, of the tribe of Benjamin, a Hebrew, [and the son] of Hebrews...."

His pride of orthodoxy, "...As to the observance of the Law I was of [the party of] the Pharisees."

Verse 6, *his pride of activity*, "As to my zeal I was a persecutor of the church...."

His pride of morality, "...By the Law's standard of righteousness — [supposed] justice, uprightness and right standing with God — I was proven to be blameless and no fault was found with me."

His response to all of this in light of the indwelling Lord Jesus? Verse 7, "...What might have been gains to me, I have come to consider as (one combined) loss for Christ's sake."

On to verse 8, "...For His sake I have lost everything and consider it all to be mere rubbish (refuse, dregs), in order that I may win (gain) Christ, the Anointed One."

What material things do you have to give up? What do I have to give up? It all pales in the presence of Paul, not to mention the Lord Jesus and what He gave up. What attitudes do we have to face and relinquish to Him? What desires and ambitions do we have that must be turned over to Him? We squirm, falter, and complain with even the slightest suggestion of turning our lives over completely to Him for whatever He might want. No, with Joel we cry, "These are mine!" They are not mine. They are not yours. They are *His*! Paul says, "Yes, indeed, they are His."

Was this all that Paul discovered when he said, "I know the secret of how to face every situation?" No, he has just begun on his exciting life which the Lord Jesus provided for him.

His second letter to the Corinthians provides incredible light, for you see, Paul didn't just discover some new facts. He hadn't just attended another seminar on the "victorious life." He had discovered the One who is Life, Jesus, and had further discovered that He was dwelling within him.

Paul said to the Thessalonians, 1st letter, verse 16, "Rejoice evermore!" The subject of the sentence? "You!" This is not a suggestion. It is not an idea. He is not creating another faith fad. This is an imperative, "Rejoice, evermore!"

Well, how does one do that? "You don't understand my situation," someone says. "No, but I know Someone who does." There is only one way that you and I can rejoice in every situation, and that is in knowing that He is in absolute control of everything that comes our way. Nothing ever takes Him by surprise.

There has never been a time when you have gone to Him in prayer explaining your situation and He responded. "Oh, I'm glad you called that to my attention, I missed that one. Thank you for reminding me. I will ponder on what to do about it and I'll get back to you." That never happens! He knows! Because He knows, we can know He knows! We can rejoice in that fact. He is more than adequate for any and all situations with which we will ever be confronted. So we can rejoice!

First Thessalonians 5:17, "Pray without ceasing!" How can we ever do that? Praying is a disposition. It is that disposition which says, "Lord Jesus, I thank You that You know what You are doing in my life. This situation has not taken You by surprise and for this I know You are adequate. For that reason, I expose this and every situation to Your complete sovereignty for You to do exactly what You want to do." Moment by moment, spread out before Him the complete facts of the circumstances. Then what?

Verse 18, "In every thing give thanks: for this is the will of God in Christ Jesus concerning you." Do what? "In everything give thanks." This is the will of God for your life, "Give thanks in and for everything."

If He knows...and He does!

If He cares...and He does!

If He is interested in us...and He is!

We can step back in utter confidence that He is in control, by faith and in the language of faith say, "Thank *You*, Lord Jesus, for Your indwelling presence. Thank You for this situation. Thank You for the way You are going to provide and work out this circumstance. I don't know when or how or where. I know nothing, but I know You! You know what to do, and my deliberate choice is, I am going to trust *You*."

What was Paul's response to his own letter to the Thessalonians? The principle is demonstrated numerous times in his second letter to the Corinthians. In Chapter 11 he is having to defend his apostleship against the false prophets and is embarrassed to have to do it. Verse 23-25 in the Amplified New Testament says, "...I am talking like one beside himself, [but] I am more, with far more extensive and abundant labors, with far more imprisonments, [beaten] with countless stripes, and frequently [at the point of] death. Five times I received from [the hands of] the Jews forty [lashes all] but one; Three times I have been beaten with rods; once I was stoned. Three times I have been aboard a ship wrecked at sea; a [whole] night and a day I have spent (adrift) on the deep."

Verses 26 through 29 continue his description of what he went through with a conspicuous absence of any complaining to his companions or to God. No disappointment with God demonstrated here. He could have complained at this point or at most any point in his life and said, "God, why is this happening to me? I have been faithful to You in sharing the Word with people, and all I ever get is rejection and rebellion, and now this physical abuse and hardship, why?" He could have complained bitterly to the Lord about his situation, but he didn't. Why? He knew the secret. What was that secret?

Look at verse 30, "If I must boast, I will boast of the things that [show] my infirmity — of the things by which I am made weak and contemptible [in the eyes of my opponents]."

Incredible! The very things that we would complain and harass God about, Paul says, "I will boast about them." It's another way of saying, "I will praise Him for these things because He knows what He is doing."

He continues in chapter 12. He speaks about having a thorn in the flesh given him so that he wouldn't get puffed up because of an experience he had. It was so painful and horrendous that "Three times I called upon the Lord and besought [Him] about this and begged that it might depart from me." Can you imagine that? It became so unbearable that he prayed about it three times. *Three times?*

We have our little difficulties and we call everyone that we know and complain bitterly to every person that will listen, and if no one will listen we head to the nearest psychiatrist and pay to have somebody listen to our woes.

Paul's situation was so difficult that he prayed about it three times. The Lord's answer is verse 9, "Paul, my grace is sufficient for you." A nice way of saying to him, "Paul, don't ever talk to Me about this again, My grace is sufficient, trust *Me!*" He did.

Paul continues in verse 9, "...Therefore, I will all the more gladly glory in my weaknesses and infirmities, that the strength and power of Christ, the Messiah, may rest — yes, may pitch a tent [over] and dwell — upon me!"

I will do what?

I will glory in my weaknesses.

I will glory in my infirmities.

This is incredible!

He is not finished.

"So for the sake of Christ, I am well pleased and take pleasure in infirmities,

"I take pleasure in insults!

"I take pleasure in hardships!

"I take pleasure in persecutions!

"I take pleasure in perplexities!

"I take pleasure in distresses!"

Why? "Because when I am weak (in human strength), then I am [truly] strong." Paul is rejoicing, and giving thanks in the adequacy and sufficiency of his indwelling Lord Jesus! *That's the secret!*

Have you ever in your life heard anyone do what Paul is describing? Quite frankly, I have heard only one or two people in nearly 50 years of ministry. How many people do you know that have entered into that kind of a relationship with the Lord Jesus? When hardship comes, they just back off and say, "Lord Jesus, thank You. You know what You are doing, and I trust You. Thank You!"

Someone said to me, "This sounds like a 'give up' mentality."

My response, "That is exactly what it is." It is an admission that we cannot live the Christian life. There has only been one person who was ever able to successfully live the Christian life. His name is Jesus. He is the only one. You can't do it, I can't do it. He alone is the one who can live the Christian life. Do you know why? He is the only one who has ever been Christ. It takes Christ to live the Christ life...the Christian life.

So...*rest! Relax!* Allow Him the right to what He bought at the cross, to not only live *in* you, but to express His life through you in any manner He chooses.

17

Fact . . . Function . . . or Fiction

Remember the TV show called "Dragnet"? The two detectives on every program in the process of interrogating someone would say, "The facts, ma'am, just the facts." The facts are not only necessary, they are imperative. For if the facts are not true, we will always reach a false conclusion. However, have we as Christians been as diligent in gathering facts that are true? Probably not, but then again, in some areas we have been very diligent.

For example, when it comes to the authority and accuracy of the Scriptures, we stand on the truth of the Word of God. When it comes to the virgin birth of the Lord Jesus, His life, death, burial, and resurrection, we stand on these truths, absolutely. On His ascension into heaven and return on the day of Pentecost, we stand, without equivocation. Absolutely the truth!

What about those truths functioning in our lives? If the Jesus who died for me, and now lives *in* me cannot somehow begin to function within me and *through* me, then for what do I need Him? Of course, we need Him when we die, that's imperative. What about daily life? Is the Christian life just a process of believing the Christian doctrines, going to church, doing our "bit" for the church and Jesus? Is that it?

Sad to say, that is about all that "it" is for many. Is this what God had in mind when He gave His only Son to die on a cross? If it is, then all the facts which we believe with incredible tenacity are nothing more than evangelical fiction.

Jesus didn't die on a cross to give us facts of history, or His story, as some have said. He gave us the facts concerning Himself in order that the facts would function within and through us. The question that looms large in my mind is, "How do these facts function?" How can I as a believer have the fact of His indwelling function within me?

Ready? Here's how! Paul, the apostle, writing to the Thessalonians in his first epistle, chapter 5, verse 18 says, "In every thing give thanks: for this is the will of God in Christ Jesus concerning you." This is not a suggestion of something we might think about as a good idea. This is an imperative, a command.

How can we possibly "Give thanks in every situation," you ask? I know of only one way. In the knowledge that He, the Lord Jesus, is in absolute control of every circumstance with which we will ever be confronted.

The Lord said to Moses through the burning bush after having been silent for 400 years, Exodus 3:7-8, "I have surely seen the affliction of my people which are in Egypt, and have heard their cry by reason of their taskmasters; for I know their sorrows; And I am come down to deliver them...." What was that again?

"I have *seen* their affliction."

"I have *heard* their cry."

"I *know* their sorrow."

"I have *seen*...I have been watching."

"I have *heard*...I have been listening."

"I *know* what you have been going through."

Who else can say anything like this? Who else has this kind of "night" vision, listening device, or knowledge? Who else can make this kind of promise, "I have come down to deliver you"?

None other that God Himself! This is the God who gave of Himself so that one day He might indwell His people. This is why we can rejoice and give thanks in every situation, not knowing the outcome; but knowing that He knows, and is in absolute control of every circumstance. We have the privilege of thanking Him in advance for what He is going to do. We can rest in His ability in response to our availability.

There is a catch. Verse 19 of 1 Thessalonians 5, "Quench not the Spirit." Ominous words. Within the context, how does one "quench the Spirit"? Quite simply, by not giving thanks. Another way to put it is to grumble and complain. We cannot give thanks and whine at the same time. It is impossible. If we want the activity of God to cease in our life, all we need to do is grumble and complain.

When I first began to discover this incredible truth I thought, "Lord, if I can't grumble and complain, what is the point in being alive? This will affect about 95 percent of my life." I thought it was my spiritual gift. That wee, small voice of the Spirit said, "I know. I know."

A classic example of this principle is found in Numbers the 12th chapter, when Miriam and Aaron talked against Moses, behind his back. Can you imagine that? Have you ever done that? Talked about someone behind their back? Criticize and gossip about them to someone else? A better question would be, do you know of anyone who hasn't done it? We all have! Not once, but many times...so what?

Read on in Numbers 12, and you will notice that God came down and talked with Miriam and Aaron, and ultimately pronounced a judgment upon Miriam. Verse 14-15, "...Let her be shut out from the camp seven days....And Miriam was shut out from the camp seven days: *and the people journeyed not* (italics mine), until Miriam was brought in again." When I first read that passage I thought, "So what," not knowing the incredible significance of their murmuring and backbiting.

Exodus 13:21 declares, "The Lord went *before* them by day in a pillar of cloud, to lead them the way; and by night in a pillar of fire, to give them light; that they might travel by day, and by night. The pillar of cloud by day, and the pillar of fire by night did not depart from before the people." They never moved unless the pillar of cloud moved. That was the *presence* of God by day and the *presence* of God by night. *The activity of God!*

For Miriam to be shut up outside the camp causing the people to "not journey onward," for the space of a week meant that the activity of God ceased, for a whole week!

God...*inactive*...for a week. For most people that wouldn't matter. You see, for most of us He hasn't ever been active. We have been too busy *for* Him to have ever entered into the reality of His activity *through* us. Most of us haven't any idea of what that is all about, but we can know.

For the most part, we have "complained" Him out of activity. I have been the worst. I was taught well, I learned well. I demonstrated it wherever I have gone. I preached it well, complaining and grumbling at every opportunity when things were not *right* in my realm of reality.

No wonder Jesus wasn't a reality in my life. He didn't have a chance. I didn't give Him an opportunity. I was too busy *for* Him, in the midst of my complaining and grumbling. However, and here is a huge HOWEVER, if grumbling and complaining *quench* the Spirit, without a doubt, rejoicing, praising and thanking will *release* the Spirit. This is why the apostle Paul constantly, as the Holy Spirit wrote through him, challenges us to rejoice and give thanks to the One who is adequate for every situation.

The Lord Jesus lives in us in His fullness and completeness (Colossians 2:9-10). The reason He lives in us, is in order that He as the vine, might flow through us as branches (John 15), and ultimately bring to fruition, through us, the fruit of the Spirit (Galatians 5:22-23).

I challenge you to face the reality of the complaining and grumbling in your life and repent, which means a 180 degree turn. Begin to rejoice and give thanks in the midst of the trials, difficulties, and stress. Thank Him for who He is, and for what He is going to do within you, to you, and through you.

The fact of who the Lord Jesus is, and who He is *in* you needn't be fiction...His plan is *function*.

Here is the plan, no longer living in the Joel mode, "these are mine." Now living in the Jesus mode, "these...my life...are *His*!"

We normally hear at this point, "May the Lord richly bless you, etc." The reality is, He has already richly blessed you with His indwelling presence, *now* thank Him! Thank Him! Thank Him!

For heaven's sake, and for your sake, thank Him!...and all of God's people said, "Amen." *No, no, no*...and all of God's people said, *"THANK YOU, LORD JESUS, FOR LIVING IN ME...THANK YOU!"*

For additional copies, write to:
   Robert G. Hobson
   10345 Sierra Dawn Drive
   Sun City, Arizona 85351
   E-mail RGHHOB@JUNO.com
   (623) 972-5421

What People Have Said

I am grateful for the teaching of the "Christ Life" that Pastor Bob Hobson proclaims. It was because of him that I came to know Christ Jesus as my Savior and life; that He lives His life through me each moment of the day. Christianity is not a religion, but the life of Christ being lived out through the believer.

Duke Snider
Baseball Hall of Fame, 1980

Some 25 years ago, I met a man who shared a message with which I was totally unfamiliar. I was a committed, hardworking Christian who had somehow totally missed the point of why Christ indwells His children. Bob shared the keys to living a joyful, abundant and victorious Christian life that are presented in this book, and I have never been the same.

My entire experience of living the Christian life changed from the position of one striving to live for Christ to one of trusting and praising Him in every situation.

These principles have revolutionized my Christian life. Therefore, I heartily recommend this volume to any and all who are frustrated or disillusioned or just worn out servants of the Lord.

Dr. Marshall Kricken
Calgary, Alberta, Canada

Bob Hobson not only has profound insights concerning the exchanged life of Christ, but he also has the unique ability to present them in a refreshing and convincing way.

The message of this book will help believers to fully appropriate the riches they have in Christ.

Dr. Lee Turner, Ph.D.
President, Grace Discipleship Ministries
Author of:
The Grace Discipleship Course and
The Advanced Grace Discipleship Course

I will always be thankful for that day in 1968 when the Lord sent me your way. How wonderful to be introduced to the living, indwelling Christ. I am so thankful to have discovered that the Christian life is not doing my best for Jesus, but rather the Lord Jesus, Himself, living in me, is capable of living His life out through me. Thank you for sharing with me and my family the truth of His indwelling.

William F. Henley, Jr.
Vice President, Director of Sales
Del Monte Corporation, Retired

Reluctantly, I attended a church in Calgary, Alberta, Canada, where Bob Hobson was the guest speaker. That evening, I not only invited Jesus Christ into my life, but I was further introduced to the reality that the Jesus who died for me, did so in order to give His life to me. I continued to discover that the reason He lived in me was in order to live His life through me. I have been spared the struggle and discouragement of the Christian life that so many go through. On a scale of one to ten...I'm at eleven!

Dr. Ron Martin
Calgary, Alberta, Canada

After receiving Jesus Christ, I desired to work for Jesus, but for years missed the simplicity of the Gospel. It not only promised forgiveness of sins and a home in heaven, but the essential truth that Jesus Christ came that I may share His life, so He could live the Christian life through me. I am grateful for Bob and Nina Hobson for sharing these truths with me.

Ruth Bock
Kinston, North Carolina

[Ruth's husband, Lew (now with the Lord) is the author of the article in Chapter 10, entitled, "The Status Quo."]